Betty Crocker

RIGHT SIZE RECIPES

Delicious Meals for One or Two

HOUGHTON MIFFLIN HARCOURT

Boston • New York

GENERAL MILLS

Global Business Solutions
Director: Heather Polen

Global Business Solutions
Manager: Andrea Kleinschmit

Executive Editor:
Cathy Swanson Wheaton

Recipe Development and Testing:
Betty Crocker Kitchens

Photography: General Mills
Photography Studios and
Image Library

HOUGHTON
MIFFLIN HARCOURT

Editorial Director: Deb Brody

Executive Editor: Anne Ficklen

Editorial Associate: Sarah Kwak

Managing Editor: Marina Padakis

Production Editor: Helen Seachrist

Art Director and Book Design:
Tai Blanche

Senior Production Coordinator:
Kimberly Kiefer

Published by Houghton Mifflin Harcourt Publishing Company.

For information about permission to reproduce selections
from this book, write to trade.permissions@hmhco.com
or to Permissions, Houghton Mifflin Harcourt Publishing Company,
3 Park Avenue, New York, New York 10016.

hmhco.com

Library of Congress Cataloging-in-Publication Data:

Names: Crocker, Betty, author.
Title: Betty Crocker right-size recipes : delicious meals for one or two.
Description: Boston : Houghton Mifflin Harcourt, 2018. | Series: BettyCrocker
    cooking | Includes index.
Identifiers: LCCN 2018038560 (print) | LCCN 2018039151 (ebook) |
    ISBN 9781328587596 (ebook) | ISBN 9781328588760 (paper over board)
Subjects: LCSH: Cooking for one. | Cooking for two. | LCGFT: Cookbooks.
Classification: LCC TX652 (ebook) | LCC TX652 .B4973 2018 (print) |
    DDC641.⅚11—dc23
LC record available at https://lccn.loc.gov/2018038560

Manufactured in China

C&C 10 9 8 7 6 5 4 3 2
4500782916

Cover photo: Sausage and Wild Mushroom
Skillet Pizza (page 136); Triple Chocolate
Skillet Brownie Sundae (page 316)

Find more great ideas at
BettyCrocker.com

Dear Reader,

We celebrate small households!

Just because you're a family of one or two doesn't mean eating has to be boring. We know taste buds get tired of eating a 4- to 6-serving recipe every night until it's gone. Grabbing takeout gets old too, or worse yet, having to throw out uneaten leftovers.

From appetizers to desserts, these right-size recipes for 1- to 2-person households are big on flavor and easy to fix, whether it's the busiest of nights or a special occasion. Skip the takeout for a home-cooked meal, know exactly what you're eating *and* have the satisfaction of making it yourself!

Getting to great taste needn't be complicated. Our kitchen-tested, easy-to-follow recipes mean delicious success every time. Look for our **5-ingredient or less recipes** and **quick-prep recipes** that take 20 minutes or less to put together. We'll show you how to cook once but eat two different meals and use up what you have on hand. We even show you how to make an entire Thanksgiving dinner for two in only 1½ hours.

Let's cook small and eat big!

Betty Crocker

CONTENTS

Cook and Bakeware for Small Households

If you're not used to cooking small batches (or cooking at all), you're not alone. The number of small households is rising, and along with it, the desire to have easy, home-cooked meals that don't require a lot of prep or cleanup.

We celebrate small households with delicious, easy-to-follow recipes that deliver big on satisfaction (from both the preparation and eating standpoints). These scaled-down recipes will delight your taste buds because you'll eat different foods all the time. They won't leave you with a pan of leftovers that you either eat every day for a week or end up throwing out!

Right-Size Equipment

Cooking for one or two is easy when you have the right-size equipment. Invest in a few pieces so you are ready to cook when the mood strikes! You'll find these pans at many discount, household goods or cooking stores as well as online.

At first, you may feel a bit like you're about to cook in a toy oven (we did!), but these small dishes will help your small-scale recipes turn out right every time. Mini-size recipes cook in less time than larger ones, cutting down time in the kitchen from larger-size recipes.

SKILLETS: You'll want to pay attention to each recipe to see if it calls for a regular or nonstick skillet. Regular skillets brown foods nicely, but we call for a nonstick skillet if the food sticks in the regular one— no one likes to have to apply elbow grease when cleaning up, if it can be avoided!

The food from cast-iron skillets usually browns nicely and releases easily due to the built-up coating that happens over time. Nonstick skillets can be substituted for the cast-iron skillets. If the recipe goes into the oven, be sure to use an ovenproof skillet as some skillets have handles that aren't intended for high oven heat.

- 6- and 8-inch regular and nonstick skillets
- 7- and 9-inch cast-iron skillets
- 10-inch skillet
- 12-inch skillet

SAUCEPANS: Saucepan sizes in the recipes are based on the amount of food that's being cooked and the ease with which to stir or add needed ingredients without making a mess.

- 1-, 2- or 3-quart regular or nonstick saucepans
- 4-quart saucepan or Dutch oven

BAKING DISHES: Baking dishes are glass or ceramic. Small dishes come in a variety of scaled-down sizes for your recipes.

- 20-ounce casserole dish
- 1-quart casserole dish
- 8-inch (2-quart) baking dish
- 9 × 5-inch (1½-quart) baking dish
- 11 × 7-inch baking dish
- 8- and 10-ounce baking dishes or ramekins (individual portion recipes)

PIE PLATES: Mini-size pie plates are perfect for individual pies or Dutch babies. Regular-size pie plates are great for the coating ingredients when coating foods like fish.

- 5½- to 6-inch pie plates
- 9-inch pie plates

BAKING PANS: Baking pans are metal. Use the smaller rimmed baking sheet when baking small, individual baking dishes, as it makes it easy to place and remove them from the oven.

- 4½ × 2½-inch mini loaf pans
- 8 × 4-inch loaf pan
- 12½ × 9½ × 1- and 15 × 10 × 1-inch rimmed baking sheets
- 8- or 9-inch square pans

CAKE PANS: Mini pans are perfect for desserts for two. Larger, shallow cake pans can also be used for coating ingredients when coating foods like fish. A small springform pan is great for small-size cheesecake and other desserts.

- 6-inch cake pan
- 8- and 9-inch cake pan
- 4½-inch springform pan

SLOW COOKERS: Slow cookers work most efficiently when they are two-thirds to three-fourths full. If you are a fan of quick, throw-together meals that cook for hours without attention, having a small-size slow cooker on hand is a must. For best results, look for slow cookers that have both low and high heat settings. Small-batch recipes typically call for 1½- to 3½-quart slow cookers.

Big Tips for Cooking Small

These kitchen-tested tips will help ensure your recipes turn out great every time:

Measuring

DRY INGREDIENTS
Measure flour and powdered sugar by spooning into a dry measuring cup and leveling off with the straight edge of a knife or metal spatula.

LIQUID INGREDIENTS
Measure liquids with a liquid (usually glass) measuring cup, or for smaller amounts, measuring teaspoons and tablespoons. Don't use flatware to measure ingredients; they aren't meant to be used as measuring tools.

GARLIC
Garlic cloves can range from very small to very large. For small-size recipes, too much or too little garlic can quickly either underflavor or overwhelm a dish! To make sure you have the correct garlic level in these recipes, we've called for measured amounts of chopped garlic rather than calling for cloves and then chopping them. Use a paring knife or mini chopper to cut them into tiny pieces so that they distribute the flavor well.

Stove-Top Savvy

PICK THE RIGHT-SIZE PAN
The wrong-size pan can affect the cooking time as well as the consistency of the food. Liquids evaporate more quickly in larger pans (causing recipes like soups and sauces to thicken more than they should, which therefore affects the yield). Foods cooked in too small of a pan (such as onions or other vegetables) can take longer to cook and steam. They are closer together; therefore, moisture cannot evaporate from them and give the edges a chance to caramelize.

CHOOSE THE BURNER
Use the correct-size burner for the pan you are using so that the cooking times are accurate and to get the best results. In general, gas flames or electric rings should not be larger than the pan. Use small burners for 1- to 2-quart saucepans and 7- to 8-inch skillets. Use large burners for saucepans larger than 2 quarts, skillets larger than 8 inches as well as Dutch ovens.

Is It Done?
Small quantities of food cook quickly! Our recipes give both the time and the doneness test to use (if possible) to help you cook and bake perfectly. Start by setting your timer for the minimum baking or cooking time given in your recipe, and then check for doneness (such as "until golden-brown" or "until center is set," etc.). If the doneness hasn't been reached, cook or bake a minute or two longer and check again.

SHOPPING SMALL
Here are some great tricks small households can use for purchasing ingredients to avoid having leftovers go to waste. Also check out our Ingredients Storage Chart (page 164) and our Use-It-Up Chart (page 238) to help you manage your kitchen pantry and refrigerator.

INGREDIENT CALLED FOR	PURCHASE
Broth	Chicken, beef or vegetable base, and reconstitute as directed on the package.
Bacon, cooked and crumbled	Look for real bacon crumbles or real bacon bits in the salad aisle of your grocery store.
Chiles in adobo sauce	Wrap any unused chiles in adobo sauce in plastic wrap like a log, about 1 inch wide. Unwrap, slice off portions and chop when you need it. 1 inch = about 1 tablespoon
Corn, cooked	Use frozen corn so that you can use just the amount you need, and keep the remaining corn in the freezer for other uses.
Juice	Look for packs of single-serve cans so you open only what you need at the time.
Meat, ground	Wrap unused ground meat in ¼- or ½-pound portions in plastic wrap and place in large freezer bag. Thaw what you need for other recipes.
Tomato paste	Drop any unused tomato paste by tablespoonfuls onto a parchment-lined plate; freeze uncovered. When frozen, transfer to a freezer bag.
Vegetables, cut, fresh	Pick up what you need at the grocery store salad bar.
Wine	Purchase one glass bottle (airline bottle–size).

NET WT. 10 OZ (283g)   K   KEEP FROZEN

CHICKEN and TURKEY

Banh Mi Pizza Panini

Prep Time: 10 Minutes • Start to Finish: 15 Minutes • 2 servings

1 frozen crisp crust cheese pizza (9.8 oz)

3 tablespoons peanut sauce

⅓ cup shredded cooked chicken

⅓ cup shredded carrot

¼ cup diced red bell pepper

2 tablespoons chopped fresh cilantro leaves

1 Heat closed contact grill or panini maker 3 to 5 minutes or according to directions. Meanwhile, unwrap pizza. Place on microwavable plate. Microwave uncovered on Defrost 2 to 3 minutes or just until pizza can be folded in half.

2 Place thawed pizza on work surface. Spread 2 tablespoons of the peanut sauce on half of pizza. Sprinkle chicken, carrot and bell pepper evenly over sauce. Fold pizza in half over filling.

3 When grill is heated, place folded pizza on grill. Close grill; cook about 5 minutes or until internal temperature reaches 160°F, crust is golden brown and cheese is melted. Remove from grill.

4 Carefully sprinkle inside with 1 tablespoon of the cilantro. Drizzle remaining peanut sauce and cilantro on top. Cut panini in half. Serve immediately.

1 Serving: Calories 470; Total Fat 20g (Saturated Fat 8g, Trans Fat 0.5g); Cholesterol 55mg; Sodium 1310mg; Total Carbohydrate 47g (Dietary Fiber 3g); Protein 26g **Exchanges:** 2 Starch, 1 Other Carbohydrate, ½ Vegetable, 1½ Lean Meat, 1 High-Fat Meat, 1½ Fat **Carbohydrate Choices:** 3

Swap It Pick your favorite brand of peanut sauce for this panini. We really enjoyed those with a hint of spice!

Kitchen Tip If you don't have a contact grill, you can "grill" this panini in a skillet over medium heat for 3 to 4 minutes per side.

Chicken *and* Poblano Sandwiches

Prep Time: 45 Minutes • Start to Finish: 45 Minutes • 2 servings (2 sandwiches each)

4 frozen crusty French or crusty wheat dinner rolls (from 12.4-oz bag)

2 boneless skinless chicken breasts (about 10 oz)

¼ teaspoon salt

¼ teaspoon dried oregano leaves

Dash freshly ground pepper

2 teaspoons olive oil

1 small poblano chile, seeded, cut into strips (about 1 cup strips)

½ small onion, sliced, separated into rings

⅓ cup refried beans (from 16-oz can)

1 small tomato, sliced

4 lettuce leaves

1 Heat oven to 425°F. Heat dinner rolls as directed on bag.

2 Place 1 chicken breast, boned side up, between 2 pieces of plastic wrap or waxed paper. Working from center, gently pound chicken with rolling pin or flat side of meat mallet until about ¼ inch thick. Repeat with remaining chicken breast. Sprinkle with salt, oregano and pepper.

3 In 10-inch skillet, heat oil over medium-high heat. Cook chicken in oil 8 to 10 minutes, turning once, until juice of chicken is clear when center of thickest part is cut (170°F). Remove from skillet; cut each in half. Cover to keep warm.

4 In same skillet, cook chile and onion over medium heat 5 to 7 minutes, stirring occasionally, until chile is crisp-tender. Meanwhile, in small microwavable bowl, microwave refried beans uncovered on High about 20 seconds or until hot.

5 With serrated knife, cut each roll in half crosswise. Spread about 1 tablespoon refried beans on bottom half of each roll. Top with chicken piece, one-fourth of pepper mixture, tomato and lettuce; cover with top half of bun.

1 Serving: Calories 450; Total Fat 12g (Saturated Fat 2.5g, Trans Fat 0g); Cholesterol 90mg; Sodium 850mg; Total Carbohydrate 44g (Dietary Fiber 4g); Protein 41g **Exchanges:** 2½ Starch, 1 Vegetable, 4½ Very Lean Meat, 1½ Fat **Carbohydrate Choices:** 3

Swap It Trade the chicken for a slice of pepper Jack cheese (omitting steps 2 and 3), and you'll have a kicked-up veggie sandwich.

Deluxe Turkey Cheeseburger Melt

Prep Time: 10 Minutes • Start to Finish: 30 Minutes • 2 servings

½   cup Bisquick™ Original mix

2   tablespoons water

1   egg white

¼   cup plus 2 tablespoons shredded Cheddar cheese (1½ oz)

¼   lb lean ground turkey

½   cup canned condensed 98% fat-free cream of mushroom soup with 30% less sodium

¾   cup frozen mixed vegetables

1 Heat oven to 400°F. Spray 8 × 4-inch loaf pan with cooking spray. In small bowl, stir Bisquick mix, water, egg white and ¼ cup of the cheese until blended; spread in pan.

2 In 10-inch skillet, cook turkey over medium-high heat, stirring occasionally, until thoroughly cooked; drain. Stir in soup and vegetables until mixture is hot. Spoon turkey mixture over batter in pan. Sprinkle with remaining 2 tablespoons cheese.

3 Bake about 20 minutes or until edges are light golden brown.

1 Serving: Calories 340 (Calories from Fat 140); Total Fat 15g (Saturated Fat 6g, Trans Fat 0g); Cholesterol 65mg; Sodium 730mg; Total Carbohydrate 29g (Dietary Fiber 2g, Sugars 4g); Protein 22g **Exchanges:** 1 Starch, 1 Other Carbohydrate, 2 Very Lean Meal, ½ High-Fat Meat, 2 Fat **Carbohydrate Choices:** 2

Swap It It's easy to substitute ¼ pound extra-lean ground beef for the turkey in this hearty main dish.

Use It Up Place the remaining soup in a small microwavable bowl; cover with plastic wrap and refrigerate. To serve for lunch the next day, add water to equal remaining soup. Heat in microwave until hot.

Slow-Cooker Mexican Chicken Tostadas

Prep Time: 20 Minutes • Start to Finish: 5 Hours 20 Minutes • 5 tostadas

½ large jalapeño chile, seeded, finely chopped

5 cloves garlic, finely chopped

1 tablespoon Mexican chili powder

1 tablespoon olive or vegetable oil

1 tablespoon lime juice

1 teaspoon salt

1 package (1¼ lb) boneless skinless chicken thighs

5 tostada shells

½ cup shredded lettuce

½ cup shredded Cheddar cheese (2 oz)

⅓ cup chunky-style salsa

Sour cream, if desired

1 In 1½-quart slow cooker, mix jalapeño chile, garlic, chili powder, oil, lime juice and salt. Add chicken; stir to mix well.

2 Cover; cook on Low heat setting 4 to 5 hours.

3 Remove chicken from cooker; place on cutting board. Shred chicken using 2 forks. Return chicken to cooker; mix well. Using slotted spoon to remove chicken mixture from cooker, place ⅓ cup chicken mixture on each tostada shell. Top with lettuce, cheese, salsa and sour cream.

1 Tostada: Calories 310; Total Fat 18g (Saturated Fat 7g, Trans Fat 0g); Cholesterol 80mg; Sodium 790mg; Total Carbohydrate 10g (Dietary Fiber 1g); Protein 27g **Exchanges:** ½ Starch, 2 Very Lean Meat, 1½ Lean Meat, 2½ Fat **Carbohydrate Choices:** ½

Kitchen Tip For an added fresh-tasting garlic kick, stir an additional finely chopped garlic clove into shredded cooked chicken.

Buffalo Chicken Chili

Prep Time: 45 Minutes • Start to Finish: 45 Minutes • 3 servings

1½ teaspoons vegetable oil

½ cup chopped onion

½ cup red or yellow bell pepper, chopped

1 cup deli rotisserie chicken, cubed

½ cup chicken broth (from 32-oz carton)

1½ teaspoons chili powder

2 or 3 drops red pepper sauce

1 can (15 oz) pinto beans, drained, rinsed

1½ cups crushed tomatoes, undrained

¾ cup diced tomatoes, undrained

¼ cup celery, sliced

¼ cup crumbled blue cheese

1 In 2-quart saucepan, heat oil over medium-high heat. Cook onion and bell pepper in oil about 5 minutes, stirring occasionally, until crisp-tender.

2 Stir in remaining ingredients except celery and blue cheese. Heat to boiling; reduce heat to medium-low. Simmer 10 to 15 minutes, stirring occasionally. Serve topped with celery and blue cheese.

1 Serving: Calories 360; Total Fat 10g (Saturated Fat 3.5g, Trans Fat 0g); Cholesterol 50mg; Sodium 1040mg; Total Carbohydrate 41g (Dietary Fiber 13g); Protein 27g **Exchanges:** 2 Starch, 2 Vegetable, 1½ Very Lean Meat, 1 Lean Meat, 1 Fat **Carbohydrate Choices:** 3

Kitchen Tip Serve the chili over hot cooked spaghetti for Cincinnati-Style Buffalo Spaghetti.

Chicken Tortilla Soup

Prep Time: 15 Minutes • Start to Finish: 20 Minutes • 3 servings

2 cups chicken broth (from 32-oz carton)

½ cup chunky-style salsa

1 cup shredded deli rotisserie chicken (from 2-lb chicken)

⅓ cup crushed tortilla chips

½ medium avocado, pitted, peeled and chopped

¾ cup shredded Monterey Jack cheese (3 oz)

1 tablespoon chopped fresh cilantro

Lime wedges, if desired

1 In 2-quart saucepan, heat broth, salsa and chicken to boiling over medium-high heat, stirring occasionally.

2 Meanwhile, divide crushed chips among 3 serving bowls. Spoon hot soup over chips; top with avocado, cheese and cilantro. Serve with lime wedges.

1 Serving: Calories 290; Total Fat 17g (Saturated Fat 7g, Trans Fat 0g); Cholesterol 65mg; Sodium 1280mg; Total Carbohydrate 11g (Dietary Fiber 2g); Protein 23g **Exchanges:** ½ Starch, 1 Very Lean Meat, 2 Lean Meat, 2 Fat **Carbohydrate Choices:** 1

Kitchen Tip Shredded corn tortillas commonly used to thicken Mexican soups are the inspiration for the crushed tortilla chip garnish.

Easy Chicken *and* Rice

Prep Time: 30 Minutes • Start to Finish: 30 Minutes • 3 servings

½ cup uncooked regular long-grain white rice

1¼ cups water

2 tablespoons olive oil

1½ cups sliced fresh mushrooms

1 cup bite-size strips red or yellow bell pepper

¼ cup green onions, finely chopped (4 medium)

1½ cloves garlic, finely chopped

½ cup tomato basil pasta sauce

¼ cup chicken broth (from 32-oz carton)

1 cup shredded deli rotisserie chicken (from 2-lb chicken)

½ cup shredded Parmesan cheese

4 teaspoons chopped fresh parsley

1 Cook rice in water as directed on package.

2 Meanwhile, in 10-inch skillet, heat oil over medium-high heat. Cook mushrooms, bell pepper, onions and garlic in oil 2 to 3 minutes, stirring frequently, until vegetables are tender. Remove from heat until rice is cooked.

3 Stir rice, pasta sauce, broth, chicken and ¼ cup of the cheese into vegetable mixture; cook over medium-low heat 3 to 5 minutes, stirring occasionally, until mixture is hot. Sprinkle with remaining ¼ cup cheese and the parsley.

1 Serving: Calories 430; Total Fat 19g (Saturated Fat 6g, Trans Fat 0g); Cholesterol 55mg; Sodium 1170mg; Total Carbohydrate 40g (Dietary Fiber 2g); Protein 25g **Exchanges:** 2 Starch, 2 Vegetable, 1 Very Lean Meat, 1 Lean Meat, 3 Fat **Carbohydrate Choices:** 2½

Use It Up Use the remaining pasta sauce from the jar over hot cooked pasta for another meal. Sprinkle each serving with shredded Parmesan cheese.

Chicken Sausage *and* Bean Soup

Prep Time: 35 Minutes • Start to Finish: 35 Minutes • 3 servings (1⅓ cups each)

1 tablespoon olive oil

2 links fully cooked chicken sausage, cut into ½-inch-thick slices

½ teaspoon finely chopped garlic

1½ cups chicken broth (from 32-oz carton)

½ cup great northern beans (from 15-oz can), drained, rinsed

½ cup sliced carrots

1 can (14.5 oz) fire-roasted diced tomatoes, undrained

1 cup chopped fresh kale

2 tablespoons Italian-style panko crispy bread crumbs

1 tablespoon grated Parmesan cheese

1 teaspoon chopped fresh basil

1 In 2-quart saucepan, heat oil over medium-high heat. Add sausage; cook and stir about 5 minutes or until sausage starts to brown. Stir in garlic; cook 30 seconds.

2 Stir in broth, beans, carrots and tomatoes; heat to boiling. Reduce heat; simmer 10 minutes. Stir in kale; cook 4 to 5 minutes longer or until carrots are tender.

3 Meanwhile, in small bowl, stir together bread crumbs, Parmesan cheese and basil. Ladle soup into serving bowls. Sprinkle each serving with crumb mixture.

1 Serving: Calories 260; Total Fat 12g (Saturated Fat 3g, Trans Fat 0g); Cholesterol 35mg; Sodium 1220mg; Total Carbohydrate 21g (Dietary Fiber 3g); Protein 15g **Exchanges:** 1 Other Carbohydrate, 1 Vegetable, 2 Lean Meat, 1 Fat **Carbohydrate Choices:** 1½

Swap It We used a chicken sausage with kale, shallots and white wine in testing, but you can use any type of cooked sausage/flavor combination in this soup.

Kitchen Tip You can purchase a head of kale or just the leaves in bags or containers. If you are purchasing a head of kale, wash leaves well and remove the tough ribs before chopping.

North Woods Wild Rice Soup

Prep Time: 20 Minutes • Start to Finish: 8 Hours 30 Minutes • 3 servings (1⅓ cups each)

1   teaspoon vegetable oil

1   small onion, chopped (½ cup)

1   medium stalk celery, diced (½ cup)

1   medium carrot, diced

½   cup diced smoked turkey (3 oz)

¼   cup uncooked wild rice

½   teaspoon dried tarragon leaves

¼   teaspoon pepper

1¾   cups chicken broth (from 32-oz carton)

½   cup frozen sweet peas, thawed

¾   cup evaporated fat-free milk (from 12-oz can)

2   tablespoons all-purpose flour

1   tablespoon dry sherry, if desired

1 In 8-inch skillet, heat oil over medium heat. Add onion; cook 3 to 4 minutes, stirring occasionally, until tender.

2 Spray 1½- to 2-quart slow cooker with cooking spray. Place onion, celery, carrot, turkey, wild rice, tarragon and pepper in cooker. Pour broth over top.

3 Cover; cook on Low heat setting 6 to 8 hours. Stir in peas for last 15 minutes of cooking.

4 In small bowl, mix milk and flour; stir into soup. Cover; cook 9 to 10 minutes or until thickened. Stir in sherry just before serving.

1 Serving: Calories 220; Total Fat 3g (Saturated Fat 0.5g, Trans Fat 0g); Cholesterol 15mg; Sodium 950mg; Total Carbohydrate 32g (Dietary Fiber 3g); Protein 16g **Exchanges:** 1½ Starch, ½ Skim Milk, ½ Vegetable, 1 Lean Meat **Carbohydrate Choices:** 2

Swap It If you have cooked chicken on hand, it's an easy swap for the turkey.

Slow-Cooker Creamy Herbed Chicken Stew

Prep Time: 15 Minutes • Start to Finish: 7 Hours 35 Minutes • 2 servings

1   cup baby-cut carrots

1   Yukon Gold potato, cut into 1½-inch pieces

¼   cup chopped onion

¼   cup sliced celery

½   teaspoon dried thyme leaves

⅛   teaspoon salt

⅛   teaspoon pepper

½   lb boneless skinless chicken thighs

¾   cup chicken broth (from 32-oz carton)

½   cup snap pea pods

¼   cup whipping cream

2   tablespoons all-purpose flour

1 Place carrots, potato, onion and celery in 2½- to 3½-quart slow cooker.

2 Sprinkle half of the thyme, the salt and pepper over vegetables in slow cooker. Place chicken on vegetables. Pour broth over top.

3 Cover and cook on Low heat setting 6 to 7 hours or until juice of chicken is clear when center of thickest part is cut (180°F) and vegetables are tender. Add pea pods; cook 5 to 10 minutes or until crisp-tender.

4 Remove chicken and vegetables from slow cooker to serving bowl using slotted spoon. Cover with foil; keep warm. Increase cooker to High heat setting. Mix whipping cream, flour and remaining thyme; stir into liquid in cooker. Cover and cook 8 to 10 minutes or until thickened. Pour over chicken and vegetables.

1 Serving: Calories 390; Total Fat 15g (Saturated Fat 7g, Trans Fat 0g); Cholesterol 145mg; Sodium 650mg; Total Carbohydrate 35g (Dietary Fiber 5g); Protein 29g **Exchanges:** 1½ Starch, 2 Vegetable, 3 Very Lean Meat, 2½ Fat **Carbohydrate Choices:** 2

Kitchen Tip If you have leftover chicken broth, try freezing it in an ice cube tray for adding to soups and stews at a later time.

Gazpacho-Style Chicken Salad

Prep Time: 25 Minutes • Start to Finish: 25 Minutes • 2 servings

SALAD

- 4 cups packed torn green and/or red leaf lettuce
- 1 package (6 oz) refrigerated grilled chicken breast strips
- 1 medium tomato, chopped (¾ cup)
- 1 cup chopped peeled cucumber
- ¾ cup chopped yellow bell pepper
- ⅓ cup thinly sliced red onion

DRESSING

- ½ cup spicy Bloody Mary mix
- 3 tablespoons red wine vinegar
- 2 tablespoons olive oil
- ½ teaspoon salt
- ¼ teaspoon pepper
- ¼ teaspoon red pepper sauce
- 1 clove garlic, finely chopped

1 Place lettuce on serving platter. Arrange chicken in mound on top of lettuce. Place remaining salad ingredients around chicken.

2 To make dressing, in tightly covered container, combine ingredients. Spoon ¼ cup dressing over salad; gently toss to coat. Serve immediately. Reserve remaining dressing for another use.

1 Serving: Calories 240; Total Fat 8g (Saturated Fat 1.5g, Trans Fat 0g); Cholesterol 70mg; Sodium 720mg; Total Carbohydrate 13g (Dietary Fiber 3g); Protein 29g **Exchanges:** 3 Vegetable, 3 Lean Meat **Carbohydrate Choices:** 1

Swap It Try white wine vinegar or cider vinegar instead of red wine vinegar.

Use It Up The remaining dressing is delicious on any salad, or drizzle on warm cooked broccoli or cauliflower.

Chicken Waldorf Salad

Prep Time: 20 Minutes • Start to Finish: 20 Minutes • 4 servings (1¼ cups each)

2 cups cubed deli rotisserie chicken (from 2-lb chicken)

2 medium unpeeled apples, cubed (2 cups)

2 medium stalks celery, sliced (1 cup)

1 cup red seedless grapes, cut in half

⅓ cup slivered almonds, toasted*

¼ cup refrigerated coleslaw dressing

4 leaves leaf lettuce

1 tablespoon thinly sliced chives

1 In large bowl, mix all ingredients except lettuce and chives.

2 On each of 4 serving plates, place 1 lettuce leaf. Spoon salad onto lettuce; sprinkle with chives.

*To toast almonds, sprinkle in ungreased heavy skillet. Cook over medium heat 5 to 7 minutes, stirring frequently until nuts begin to brown, then stirring constantly until nuts are light brown. To toast nuts in the oven, heat oven to 350°F. Spread nuts in ungreased shallow pan. Bake, uncovered, 6 to 10 minutes, stirring occasionally, until light brown.

1 Serving: Calories 290; Total Fat 13g (Saturated Fat 2.5g, Trans Fat 0g); Cholesterol 65mg; Sodium 510mg; Total Carbohydrate 21g (Dietary Fiber 4g); Protein 22g **Exchanges:** 1 Fruit, 1½ Vegetable, 2½ Lean Meat, 1 Fat **Carbohydrate Choices:** 1½

Kitchen Tip The newly created Waldorf Salad was the talk of socialites who dined at New York's Waldorf-Astoria Hotel in the 1890s. This contemporary version will delight your guests just as much.

Gluten-Free Buffalo Chicken Salad

Prep Time: 20 Minutes • Start to Finish: 45 Minutes • 4 servings

CHICKEN

- 1 teaspoon butter
- ¼ cup red pepper wing sauce
- 1 teaspoon celery seed
- 2 boneless skinless chicken breasts (about ¾ lb)

DRESSING

- ½ cup plain nonfat Greek yogurt
- 2 tablespoons light mayonnaise
- 1 teaspoon gluten-free Worcestershire sauce
- ½ teaspoon pepper
- ¼ teaspoon sugar
- 1 tablespoon lemon juice
- 1 tablespoon water
- 1 clove garlic, finely chopped
- 2 tablespoons finely chopped chives
- 2 tablespoons finely chopped parsley

SALAD

- 1 bag (10 oz) chopped hearts of romaine lettuce (about 6 cups)
- 1 cup shredded carrots
- 1½ cups cherry tomatoes, cut in half
- 2 tablespoons crumbled blue cheese

1 Heat oven to 425°F. Line cookie sheet with foil. Spray foil with cooking spray; set aside. In medium microwavable bowl, microwave butter on High 30 to 45 seconds or until melted. Add wing sauce and celery seed; stir to combine. Reserve 2 tablespoons sauce mixture in small bowl; set aside.

2 Add chicken breasts to remaining sauce mixture; toss to coat. Place chicken on cookie sheet. Bake 15 to 20 minutes or until juice of chicken is clear when center of thickest part is cut (at least 165°F).

3 In large bowl, beat all dressing ingredients except chives and parsley; refrigerate until just before serving.

4 Stir chives and parsley into dressing. Toss lettuce and carrots in dressing. Divide mixture among 4 plates. Top with tomatoes.

5 Transfer chicken breasts to cutting board; thinly slice. Divide chicken evenly over salads. Drizzle reserved marinade over chicken; top with blue cheese.

1 Serving: Calories 230; Total Fat 9g (Saturated Fat 3g, Trans Fat 0g); Cholesterol 60mg; Sodium 410mg, Total Carbohydrate 12g (Dietary Fiber 3g); Protein 24g **Exchanges:** 2½ Vegetable, 2½ Very Lean Meat, 1½ Fat **Carbohydrate Choices:** 1

Swap It Don't have celery seed in the spice rack? You can opt to leave it out of the sauce and add some chopped fresh celery to the salad, if desired.

Kitchen Tip This chicken is great cold too. Try shredding and tucking into a gluten-free pita or wrap with some of the dressed salad.

Chicken *and* Berry Salad

Prep Time: 15 Minutes • Start to Finish: 15 Minutes • 3 servings

- 1 package (6 oz) refrigerated grilled chicken strips, cut in half if necessary
- 5 cups bite-size pieces mixed salad greens
- 1 cup strawberry halves
- ½ cup blueberries
- ½ cup raspberries
- ¼ cup honey-roasted peanuts
- ¼ cup vinaigrette dressing
- 2 tablespoons crumbled blue cheese

In large bowl, combine all ingredients except vinaigrette and blue cheese. Toss gently with vinaigrette to mix. Sprinkle with blue cheese. Serve immediately.

1 Serving: Calories 260; Total Fat 13g (Saturated Fat 3g, Trans Fat 0g); Cholesterol 45mg; Sodium 640mg; Total Carbohydrate 18g (Dietary Fiber 5g); Protein 18g **Exchanges:** 1 Fruit, 1 Vegetable, 2 Very Lean Meat, ½ High-Fat Meat, 1½ Fat **Carbohydrate Choices:** 1

Swap It If you prefer a fruitier flavor, you can use raspberry vinaigrette in place of regular vinaigrette.

Kitchen Tip Summer is a great time to use all the different varieties of garden greens. If you're looking to save time, though, use 5 cups from a purchased bag of torn mixed greens.

Menu

Roast Turkey

—

Roasted Potatoes
with Gravy

—

Green Beans
with Mushrooms

—

Roasted Sweet Potatoes

Scaled-Down Turkey Dinner Game Plan:

1 Prep the stuffing. Use a stuffing mix or make our irresistible Butternut Squash and Leek Stuffing (page 301).

2 Begin roasting the turkey, potatoes and sweet potatoes. Place them on the pan next to the turkey.

3 Prep the green bean mixture. It's green beans, mushrooms and onions—yum!

4 Place the green beans on the other side of the turkey, and the stuffing in a foil pouch next to the pan in the oven.

5 Season turkey and veggies. Different seasonings go on the different foods for a variety of flavors.

6 Place the turkey, veggies and stuffing on plates or in bowls for serving; keep warm. Make gravy with drippings from the pan.

7 Enjoy!

Thanksgiving on Your Table in 1½ Hours

Our Sheet Pan Turkey Dinner is a cleverly orchestrated recipe that minimizes your prep and cleanup time. You don't have to get up at the crack of dawn to start your turkey, and you won't have endless leftovers. All you need to add are rolls and dessert.

Sheet Pan Turkey Dinner

Prep Time: 30 Minutes • Start to Finish: 1 Hour 30 Minutes • 3 servings

3 tablespoons vegetable oil

1 package (6 oz) stuffing mix

1 bone-in turkey breast half (1¾ to 2¼ lb)

6 red-skinned baby potatoes, cut in half (8 oz)

1 medium dark-orange sweet potato, peeled, cut lengthwise in half

6 oz fresh green beans, trimmed

8 medium fresh mushrooms, halved

¼ cup thinly sliced onion

½ teaspoon salt

¼ teaspoon pepper

¼ teaspoon dried rosemary, crushed or 1 teaspoon chopped fresh rosemary

¼ teaspoon dried Italian seasoning

2 teaspoons packed brown sugar

¾ cup water

1 tablespoon plus 2 teaspoons all-purpose flour

1. Heat oven to 400°F. Brush 15 × 10 × 1-inch pan with 1 tablespoon of the oil. Make stuffing mix as directed on package; set aside.

2. Place turkey, skin side up, in center of pan. In medium bowl, toss potatoes and sweet potato with 1 tablespoon of the oil. Arrange in single layer on one side of turkey on pan. Rub any oil remaining in bowl over turkey.

3. Bake, uncovered, 30 minutes.

4. Meanwhile, in medium bowl, mix green beans, mushrooms and onion with remaining 1 tablespoon oil. Cut 12 × 12-inch piece of foil. Place 2 cups of stuffing in center of foil. (Cover and refrigerate remaining stuffing for another meal.) Bring up 2 sides of foil so edges meet. Seal edges, making tight ½-inch fold. Fold other sides to seal.

5. Remove pan from oven. Turn potatoes and sweet potatoes over. Arrange green bean mixture in single layer on other side of turkey. Sprinkle vegetables and turkey with salt and pepper. Sprinkle potatoes with rosemary and turkey with Italian seasoning. Return to oven. Place stuffing packet on oven rack next to pan.

6. Bake 25 to 40 minutes longer or until thermometer inserted in center of turkey reads 165°F. Remove pan from oven. Place turkey on cutting board; cover with foil to keep warm. Remove vegetables to separate ovenproof serving bowls. Sprinkle brown sugar onto sweet potatoes; cover with foil. Cover green beans and potatoes with foil.

7. Pour ½ cup of the water onto pan; mix with pancake turner and scrape to remove browned bits and drippings from pan; scrape mixture into 1-quart saucepan. Heat to boiling. In small bowl, stir flour and remaining ¼ cup water. Stir into boiling broth with whisk. Cook and stir 1 to 2 minutes or until slightly thickened. Slice turkey crosswise into slices. Serve with vegetables, stuffing and gravy.

Swap It Use Butternut Squash and Leek Stuffing (page 301) for the prepared stuffing. Prepare through step 2 and continue as directed.

1 Serving: Calories 760; Total Fat 29g (Saturated Fat 10g, Trans Fat 1g); Cholesterol 160mg; Sodium 1210mg; Total Carbohydrate 63g (Dietary Fiber 6g); Protein 60g **Exchanges:** 3½ Starch, 2½ Vegetable, 6½ Lean Meat, 1½ Fat **Carbohydrate Choices:** 4

Greek *and* Chicken Pasta

Prep Time: 30 Minutes • Start to Finish: 55 Minutes • 3 servings

1 cup uncooked penne pasta (4 oz)

2 tablespoons butter

½ cup chopped onion

2 tablespoons all-purpose flour

1 cup reduced-sodium chicken broth (from 32-oz carton)

½ cup crumbled feta cheese (2 oz)

1½ cups chopped deli rotisserie chicken (from 2-lb chicken)

⅓ cup marinated artichoke hearts, drained, chopped

¼ cup sun-dried tomatoes in oil, drained, chopped

2 tablespoons sliced kalamata olives

1 tablespoon chopped fresh parsley

1 Heat oven to 350°F. Spray 20-ounce casserole dish with cooking spray. Cook and drain pasta as directed on package.

2 Meanwhile, in 2-quart saucepan, melt butter over medium heat. Add onion; cook 3 minutes, stirring occasionally. Stir in flour; cook and stir 30 seconds. Slowly stir in broth; heat to boiling. Cook 3 to 4 minutes, stirring frequently, until thickened. Remove from heat; stir in cheese. Gently stir in cooked pasta, chicken, artichoke hearts, tomatoes, olives and parsley. Spoon into casserole dish.

3 Bake, uncovered, 25 to 30 minutes or until hot. Garnish with additional fresh parsley, if desired.

1 Serving: Calories 520; Total Fat 22g (Saturated Fat 11g, Trans Fat 0.5g); Cholesterol 105mg; Sodium 920mg; Total Carbohydrate 48g (Dietary Fiber 4g); Protein 32g **Exchanges:** 2 Starch, 1 Other Carbohydrate, ½ Vegetable, 3 Lean Meat, ½ Medium-Fat Meat, 2 Fat **Carbohydrate Choices:** 3

Use It Up Any leftover sun-dried tomatoes or artichoke hearts are wonderful when added to almost any salad.

Tarragon *and* Chicken Pasta

Prep Time: 25 Minutes • Start to Finish: 25 Minutes • 2 servings

¾ cup uncooked mostaccioli pasta (2¼ oz)

1 cup sliced mushrooms (3 oz)

½ cup broccoli florets

1 medium carrot, thinly sliced (½ cup)

½ cup fat-free (skim) milk

1½ teaspoons cornstarch

1 teaspoon chopped fresh or ¼ teaspoon dried tarragon leaves

⅛ teaspoon salt

1 clove garlic, finely chopped

1 cup shredded spinach or romaine (1¼ oz)

¾ cup cut-up cooked chicken or turkey

¼ cup shredded reduced-fat Swiss cheese (1 oz)

1 In 3-quart saucepan, cook pasta as directed on package, adding mushrooms, broccoli and carrot during last 4 minutes of cooking. Drain; return pasta and vegetables to saucepan. Cover to keep warm.

2 Meanwhile, in 1½-quart saucepan, mix milk, cornstarch, tarragon, salt and garlic. Cook over medium heat, stirring constantly, until mixture thickens and boils. Stir in remaining ingredients until cheese is melted and spinach is wilted. Pour over pasta and vegetables; toss to combine.

1 Serving: Calories 400; Total Fat 7g (Saturated Fat 2g, Trans Fat 0g); Cholesterol 50mg; Sodium 800mg; Total Carbohydrate 53g (Dietary Fiber 4g); Protein 30g **Exchanges:** 3 Starch, 2 Vegetable, 2 Very Lean Meat, ½ High-Fat Meat **Carbohydrate Choices:** 3½

Swap It You can use a different pasta instead of mostaccioli. You will need about 1 cup elbow macaroni to equal 4 ounces, or about 2 cups egg noodles.

Swap It Change the flavor by switching spice. Cilantro, marjoram or parsley are good substitutes for tarragon.

Spicy Chicken Enchiladas

Prep Time: 25 Minutes • Start to Finish: 1 Hour 5 Minutes • 2 servings

1 boneless skinless chicken breast half, cut into bite-size pieces

¼ cup chopped onion

¼ teaspoon dried oregano leaves

⅛ teaspoon salt

Dash pepper

¼ cup shredded Monterey Jack cheese (1 oz)

¼ cup sour cream

1 tablespoon chopped green chiles (from 4.5-oz can)

¾ cup enchilada sauce (from 10-oz can)

2 flour tortillas (8 inch)

¼ cup shredded Cheddar cheese (1 oz)

¼ cup chopped lettuce

¼ cup chopped tomato

1 Heat oven to 350°F. Spray 9 × 5-inch (1½-quart) glass loaf dish with nonstick cooking spray. Spray 10-inch skillet with cooking spray. Add chicken to skillet; cook and stir over medium-high heat 2 to 3 minutes or until lightly browned.

2 Add onion, oregano, salt and pepper; cook and stir 3 to 5 minutes or until chicken is no longer pink in center. Remove from heat; cool 5 minutes. Stir in Monterey Jack cheese, sour cream and chiles.

3 Spread ¼ cup of the enchilada sauce in bottom of loaf dish. Spoon half of chicken mixture evenly down center of each tortilla; roll up. Place filled tortillas, seam side down, over sauce in dish. Spoon remaining ½ cup enchilada sauce over tortillas. Cover with foil.

4 Bake 25 to 30 minutes or until thoroughly heated. Uncover; sprinkle with Cheddar cheese. Bake an additional 4 to 5 minutes or until cheese is melted. To serve, sprinkle with lettuce and tomato.

1 Serving: Calories 460; Total Fat 22g (Saturated Fat 10g, Trans Fat 0.5g); Cholesterol 95mg; Sodium 1230mg; Total Carbohydrate 35g (Dietary Fiber 4g); Protein 31g **Exchanges:** 2 Starch, 1 Vegetable, 3 Very Lean Meat, 4 Fat **Carbohydrate Choices:** 2

Use It Up Heat the remaining enchilada sauce to serve with the baked enchiladas or as dip for chips!

Chicken *and* Corn Quesadillas

Prep Time: 15 Minutes • Start to Finish: 35 Minutes • 2 servings

2 flour tortillas (10 inch)

1 tablespoon butter, melted

2 tablespoons sour cream

2 tablespoons chunky-style salsa

½ cup shredded cooked chicken

¾ cup shredded Mexican cheese blend (3 oz)

¼ cup frozen corn, thawed

2 tablespoons sliced green onions (2 medium)

1 Heat oven to 400°F. Brush 1 side of each tortilla with butter. Place 1 tortilla on ungreased large cookie sheet, butter side down.

2 In small bowl, mix sour cream and salsa. Spread about 1½ tablespoons of the sour cream mixture over tortilla on cookie sheet. Top with chicken, 1 tablespoon of the cheese, the corn and onions. Sprinkle with remaining cheese. Place remaining tortilla, butter side up, over filling; press gently.

3 Bake 15 to 18 minutes or until cheese is melted and top is light golden brown. To serve, cut into wedges. Serve with additional salsa, if desired.

1 Serving: Calories 560; Total Fat 31g (Saturated Fat 16g, Trans Fat 1.5g); Cholesterol 100mg; Sodium 910mg; Total Carbohydrate 43g (Dietary Fiber 2g); Protein 27g **Exchanges:** 2½ Starch, ½ Other Carbohydrate, 2½ Medium-Fat Meat, 3 Fat **Carbohydrate Choices:** 3

Swap It Any cooked meat can be substituted for the chicken in this Southwest favorite.

Swap It You could use Colby–Monterey Jack or Cheddar cheese instead of the Mexican cheese blend.

One-Pot Creamy Chicken Spaghetti

Prep Time: 45 Minutes • Start to Finish: 45 Minutes • 2 servings

1 boneless skinless chicken breast, cut into 1-inch pieces

1 teaspoon Italian seasoning

¼ teaspoon crushed red pepper flakes

1 tablespoon butter

1 cup thinly sliced fresh mushrooms

¼ lb uncooked spaghetti, broken in half

2 cups chicken broth (from 32-oz carton)

¼ cup whipping cream

1 clove garlic, finely chopped

2 cups fresh baby spinach leaves

¼ cup shredded Parmesan cheese

½ teaspoon lemon juice

1 In small bowl, toss chicken, Italian seasoning and pepper flakes.

2 In 4-quart saucepan, melt butter over medium-high heat. Add chicken; cook 2 minutes without stirring, until browned on first side. Stir and turn chicken. Add mushrooms; cook 4 to 6 minutes longer, stirring frequently, until mushrooms are tender.

3 Add spaghetti, broth, whipping cream and garlic. Heat just to boiling over high heat. Reduce heat to medium; cook 12 to 16 minutes, stirring frequently, until spaghetti is cooked. Stir in spinach and 2 tablespoons of the Parmesan cheese. Remove from heat; let stand 1 minute. Stir in lemon juice. Top individual servings with remaining 2 tablespoons Parmesan cheese.

1 Serving: Calories 590; Total Fat 25g (Saturated Fat 14g, Trans Fat 1g); Cholesterol 115mg; Sodium 1150mg; Total Carbohydrate 55g (Dietary Fiber 4g); Protein 36g **Exchanges:** 3 Starch, ½ Other Carbohydrate, 1 Vegetable, 3 Very Lean Meat, ½ Lean Meat, 4 Fat **Carbohydrate Choices:** 3½

Kitchen Tip Stir, stir, stir! One-pots cook quickly, so be sure to stir frequently to prevent the pasta from sticking to the pan.

Kitchen Tip It's okay to increase or decrease the pepper flakes per your own taste preferences.

Chicken Schnitzel *with* Arugula *and* Tomato Salad

Prep Time: 25 Minutes • Start to Finish: 25 Minutes • 2 servings

2 boneless skinless chicken breasts

½ teaspoon salt

½ teaspoon pepper

¼ cup all-purpose flour

2 eggs

⅔ cup plain panko crispy bread crumbs

3 tablespoons olive oil

1 teaspoon lemon juice

2 cups packed baby arugula leaves (about 2 oz)

½ cup cherry tomatoes, halved

Lemon wedges

1 Between pieces of plastic wrap or waxed paper, place each chicken breast smooth side down; gently pound with flat side of meat mallet or rolling pin until about ¼ inch thick. Sprinkle chicken with ¼ teaspoon of the salt and ¼ teaspoon of the pepper.

2 In shallow bowl, stir together flour, remaining ¼ teaspoon salt and ¼ teaspoon pepper. Coat both sides of chicken with flour mixture. Beat eggs in shallow bowl with whisk. Place bread crumbs in another shallow bowl. Dip chicken into beaten eggs; turn to coat. Coat in bread crumbs, covering completely.

3 In 12-inch nonstick skillet, heat 2 tablespoons of the oil over medium heat. Add chicken; cook 6 to 8 minutes, turning once, until no longer pink in center. Place chicken on serving plates.

4 Meanwhile, in small bowl, stir remaining oil and the lemon juice. Add arugula and tomatoes; stir gently to mix. Serve with chicken; top with lemon wedges.

1 Serving: Calories 660; Total Fat 33g (Saturated Fat 6g, Trans Fat 0g); Cholesterol 290mg; Sodium 1330mg; Total Carbohydrate 42g (Dietary Fiber 1g); Protein 48g **Exchanges:** 2 Starch, ½ Other Carbohydrate, 1½ Vegetable, 4½ Lean Meat, 1 Medium-Fat Meat, 2½ Fat **Carbohydrate Choices:** 3

Swap It Arugula is a variety of lettuce with a peppery flavor. Mixed baby lettuce would work well in this recipe as a substitute.

Kitchen Tip Pounding the chicken gives it a uniform thickness, which helps the chicken cook evenly.

Chicken Tomato Curry With Coconut Quinoa

Prep Time: 40 Minutes • Start to Finish: 40 Minutes • 2 servings (¾ cup quinoa, 1½ cups curry each)

COCONUT QUINOA

- ½ cup uncooked quinoa, rinsed, well drained
- ¾ cup unsweetened coconut milk (from 13.66-oz can)
- ¼ cup water
- ¼ teaspoon salt
- 2 tablespoons chopped fresh cilantro

CURRY

- 1 teaspoon vegetable oil
- ½ lb boneless skinless chicken thighs, cut into bite-size pieces (1½ cups)
- ½ cup sliced onion (1 small)
- ½ medium green bell pepper, cut into 1x¼-inch strips (½ cup)
- 2 teaspoons finely chopped garlic
- 1 can (14.5 oz) fire-roasted diced tomatoes, undrained
- ⅓ cup raisins
- 2 to 2½ teaspoons curry powder
- ¼ teaspoon ground nutmeg
- ¼ teaspoon salt
- 2 tablespoons sliced almonds
- 1 tablespoon fresh cilantro leaves

1 In 1-quart saucepan, combine quinoa, coconut milk, water and ¼ teaspoon salt. Cover; heat to boiling. Reduce heat; simmer 12 to 15 minutes or until liquid is absorbed. Stir in 2 tablespoons cilantro.

2 Meanwhile, in 10-inch nonstick skillet, heat oil over medium-high heat. Add chicken; cook 4 to 5 minutes, stirring occasionally, until browned.

3 Reduce heat to medium. Add onion and bell pepper; cook 2 minutes, stirring frequently. Add garlic; cook 1 minute, stirring constantly.

4 Add tomatoes, raisins, curry powder, nutmeg and ¼ teaspoon salt. Heat to boiling; reduce heat to low. Simmer 10 to 15 minutes, stirring occasionally, until chicken is no longer pink in center.

5 Serve curry over quinoa. Top each serving with half of the almonds and cilantro leaves.

1 Serving: Calories 670; Total Fat 29g (Saturated Fat 16g, Trans Fat 0g); Cholesterol 110mg; Sodium 1000mg; Total Carbohydrate 67g (Dietary Fiber 9g); Protein 35g **Exchanges:** 2 Starch, ½ Fruit, 1½ Other Carbohydrate, 2 Vegetable, 3 Very Lean Meat, ½ High-Fat Meat, 4½ Fat **Carbohydrate Choices:** 4½

Swap It If you have boneless chicken breasts, you can use them in place of the chicken thighs.

Use It Up See page 164 for how to store leftover coconut milk. Use it in smoothies, soups, marinades or curries.

Kitchen Tip Curry powder is actually a blend of herbs, spices and seeds, which is why the flavor of different brands can vary dramatically. There is often a sweet version that is milder than the hot version, which has a little kick.

CHICKEN AND TURKEY

Lemon-Apricot Chicken

Prep Time: 20 Minutes • Start to Finish: 45 Minutes • 3 servings

2 tablespoons butter, melted

1 egg

⅓ cup all-purpose flour

2 teaspoons grated lemon peel

½ teaspoon garlic salt

3 boneless skinless chicken breasts

⅓ cup apricot preserves

1 tablespoon lemon juice

¼ teaspoon soy sauce

¼ teaspoon ground ginger

Lemon slices, if desired

1 Heat oven to 425°F. Brush 15 × 10 × 1-inch pan with melted butter. In shallow dish, beat egg. In another shallow dish, stir flour, lemon peel and garlic salt.

2 Between pieces of plastic wrap or waxed paper, place each chicken breast; gently pound with flat side of meat mallet or rolling pin until about ½ inch thick. Dip chicken into egg, then coat with flour mixture; place in pan.

3 Bake, uncovered, 10 minutes. Turn; bake 10 to 15 minutes longer or until juice of chicken is clear when thickest part is cut (165°F).

4 In small microwavable bowl, stir all remaining ingredients except lemon slices. Microwave on High 1 minute; stir. Cut chicken crosswise into ½-inch slices. Pour sauce over chicken. Garnish with lemon slices.

1 Serving: Calories 440; Total Fat 15g (Saturated Fat 7g, Trans Fat 0g); Cholesterol 185mg; Sodium 370mg; Total Carbohydrate 36g (Dietary Fiber 1g); Protein 41g **Exchanges:** 1½ Starch, 1 Other Carbohydrate, 5 Lean Meat **Carbohydrate Choices:** 2½

Oven-Roasted Chicken *and* Vegetables

Prep Time: 10 Minutes • Start to Finish: 35 Minutes • 2 servings

1   cup ready-to-eat baby-cut carrots, cut in half lengthwise

1   cup frozen potato wedges with skins

½   cup frozen whole green beans

½   cup frozen bell pepper and onion stir-fry

½   cup grape tomatoes

1½ tablespoons olive or vegetable oil

¼   teaspoon seasoned salt

1   deli rotisserie chicken, cut into serving pieces

1 Heat oven to 475°F. In large bowl, toss all ingredients except chicken.

2 In ungreased 13 × 9-inch pan, arrange chicken and vegetables in single layer.

3 Bake, uncovered, 20 to 25 minutes or until vegetables are crisp-tender and chicken is hot.

1 Serving: Calories 470; Total Fat 23g (Saturated Fat 5g, Trans Fat 0g); Cholesterol 150mg; Sodium 1110mg; Total Carbohydrate 15g (Dietary Fiber 4g); Protein 51g **Exchanges:** ½ Starch, 2 Vegetable, 3 Very Lean Meat, 3½ Lean Meat, 2 Fat **Carbohydrate Choices:** 1

Swap It Rotisserie chickens are often available in flavors. Choose any flavor for this recipe.

Orange Chicken *with* Snow Peas *and* Carrots

Prep Time: 50 Minutes • Start to Finish: 50 Minutes • 2 servings

CHICKEN

- 2 boneless skinless chicken breasts, cut into 1½-inch pieces
- 1 teaspoon soy sauce
- ¼ cup cornstarch
- ½ cup vegetable oil for frying

SAUCE

- ⅓ cup orange juice
- 2 teaspoons cornstarch
- 1 tablespoon vegetable oil
- 2 cloves garlic, finely chopped
- 2 teaspoons finely chopped fresh gingerroot
- 1 teaspoon grated orange peel
- ¼ teaspoon crushed red pepper flakes
- ½ cup chicken broth (from 32-oz carton)
- 2 teaspoons soy sauce
- 2 teaspoons unseasoned rice vinegar
- 2 tablespoons sugar

VEGETABLES

- 1 tablespoon vegetable oil
- 3 oz snow peas, sliced (about 1 cup)
- 2 medium carrots, thinly sliced

1 In medium bowl, toss chicken pieces and soy sauce. In small bowl, beat orange juice and 2 teaspoons cornstarch with whisk until cornstarch is dissolved. Line 15 × 10 × 1-inch pan with paper towels.

2 In 10-inch skillet, heat 1 tablespoon oil over medium heat. Add garlic, gingerroot, orange peel and pepper flakes; stir-fry about 30 seconds or until fragrant. Add broth, 2 teaspoons soy sauce, the vinegar and sugar; stir about 30 seconds or until sugar dissolves. Stir orange juice mixture, then add it to skillet. Heat sauce to boiling, stirring. Reduce heat to low; simmer 1 minute. Transfer sauce to bowl; wipe out skillet.

3 Place ¼ cup cornstarch in shallow bowl. Toss chicken in cornstarch, coating evenly and gently knocking off any excess; transfer to plate.

4 In 4-quart Dutch oven, heat ½ cup vegetable oil over medium-high heat. Carefully add coated chicken to hot oil, spacing pieces apart from each other. Fry chicken 5 to 7 minutes, turning once or twice, until deep golden. Using slotted spoon, transfer chicken to pan.

5 In same 10-inch skillet used for sauce, heat 1 tablespoon oil over medium heat. Add snow peas and carrots; cook 3 to 4 minutes, stirring frequently, until vegetables are just tender. Add chicken and reserved sauce; stir until heated through and thoroughly coated in sauce.

1 Serving: Calories 580; Total Fat 27g (Saturated Fat 5g, Trans Fat 0g); Cholesterol 100mg; Sodium 780mg; Total Carbohydrate 46g (Dietary Fiber 3g); Protein 40g **Exchanges:** 1 Starch, 1½ Other Carbohydrate, 2 Vegetable, 4½ Lean Meat, 2½ Fat **Carbohydrate Choices:** 3

Swap It One cup green beans, cut into 2-inch pieces, make a nice substitute for the snow peas in this recipe.

Kitchen Tip Steamed white rice makes a nice accompaniment to this dish.

Pineapple Chicken Salad Lettuce Wraps

Prep Time: 15 Minutes • Start to Finish: 15 Minutes • 2 servings (3 wraps each)

1 container (6 oz) pineapple yogurt

¼ teaspoon salt

¼ teaspoon pepper

1½ cups chopped cooked chicken

¼ cup shredded carrot

2 tablespoons sliced green onions (2 medium)

2 tablespoons chopped red bell pepper

2 tablespoons chopped celery

6 leaves Bibb lettuce

1 In medium bowl, mix yogurt, salt and pepper. Stir in all remaining ingredients except lettuce until combined.

2 Divide chicken mixture evenly among lettuce leaves (about ⅓ cup per leaf). Serve immediately.

1 Serving: Calories 270; Total Fat 7g (Saturated Fat 3g, Trans Fat 0g); Cholesterol 95mg; Sodium 430mg; Total Carbohydrate 16g (Dietary Fiber 1g); Protein 34g **Exchanges:** 1 Starch, 4½ Very Lean Meat, 1 Fat **Carbohydrate Choices:** 1

Swap It Try serving the chicken salad on whole wheat bread or inside a pita pocket instead of as a lettuce wrap.

Kitchen Tip Add 2 teaspoons finely chopped fresh jalapeño chile to the chicken salad to add a little heat.

Salsa Chicken Fiesta Bake

Prep Time: 15 Minutes • Start to Finish: 40 Minutes • 2 servings

⅓ cup Original Bisquick mix

1 tablespoon water

1 egg white

¼ cup plus 2 tablespoons shredded Cheddar cheese (1½ oz)

2 teaspoons vegetable oil

1 boneless skinless chicken breast, cut into ½-inch pieces

½ cup chunky-style salsa

2 tablespoons thinly sliced green onions

1 Heat oven to 400°F. Line 8 × 4-inch loaf pan with foil, leaving foil overhanging at 2 opposite sides of pan; spray foil with cooking spray. In small bowl, stir Bisquick mix, water and egg white; spread in pan. Sprinkle with ¼ cup of the cheese.

2 In 10-inch nonstick skillet, heat oil. Cook chicken over medium-high heat, stirring frequently, until no longer pink; drain. Stir in salsa; heat until hot. Spoon over batter in pan to within ½ inch of edges.

3 Bake 16 to 18 minutes. Sprinkle with remaining 2 tablespoons cheese. Bake about 2 minutes longer or until cheese is melted. Sprinkle with green onions.

1 Serving: Calories 320; Total Fat 15g (Saturated Fat 5g, Trans Fat 0g); Cholesterol 70mg; Sodium 820mg; Total Carbohydrate 18g (Dietary Fiber 1g); Protein 26g **Exchanges:** ½ Starch, ½ Other Carbohydrate, 3 Very Lean Meat, ½ High-Fat Meat, 2 Fat **Carbohydrate Choices:** 1

Swap It You can use 2 cups precooked chicken instead of the chicken breast. Just omit the oil for cooking the chicken and heat the cooked chicken with the salsa.

Puff Pastry Chicken Pot Pies

Prep Time: 30 Minutes • Start to Finish: 50 Minutes • 2 servings

1 tablespoon plus
1 teaspoon butter

1 cup chopped mushrooms

½ cup French green beans
(haricots verts), cut into
½-inch pieces

¼ cup diced shallots
or onion

2 tablespoons all-
purpose flour

⅛ teaspoon dried
thyme leaves

⅛ teaspoon pepper

½ cup water

⅓ cup milk

½ teaspoon roasted chicken
base (from 8-oz jar)

1 cup chopped cooked
chicken

1 can (7 oz) petite artichoke
hearts, drained, chopped

2 frozen puff pastry cups
(from 10-oz package)

1 teaspoon grated
Parmesan cheese

1 teaspoon chopped Italian
(flat-leaf) parsley

1 Heat oven to 425°F. Spray 2 (8-ounce) custard cups or ramekins with cooking spray. Place cups on 12½ × 9½ × 1-inch pan.

2 In 10-inch nonstick skillet, melt 1 tablespoon of the butter over medium heat; add mushrooms, beans and shallots. Cook 3 to 5 minutes or until vegetables are tender. Sprinkle with flour, thyme and pepper; stir until coated. Add water, milk, chicken base, chicken and artichokes; cook over medium heat, stirring frequently, 2 to 3 minutes or until thickened and bubbly. Divide chicken mixture between custard cups; cover with foil to keep filling warm.

3 In small microwavable bowl, microwave remaining 1 teaspoon butter on High 5 to 10 seconds until melted. Place puff pastry cups on cookie sheet next to custard cups. Brush tops of pastry cups with melted butter; sprinkle with cheese and parsley.

4 Bake filling covered and pastry cups uncovered 14 to 19 minutes or until pastry is puffed and golden brown. Remove foil from filling; top with baked pastry shells.

1 Serving: Calories 540; Total Fat 28g (Saturated Fat 9g, Trans Fat 4.5g); Cholesterol 80mg; Sodium 740mg; Total Carbohydrate 42g (Dietary Fiber 7g); Protein 29g **Exchanges:** 2 Starch, 2½ Vegetable, 2½ Lean Meat, 4 Fat **Carbohydrate Choices:** 3

Swap It If you can't find thin French green beans, regular fresh green beans can be used as a substitute.

Use It Up Keep remaining pastry cups in freezer. For an easy dessert, bake shells and cool completely. Fill with fresh fruit and whipped topping and garnish with chocolate shavings.

Kitchen Tip Chicken base is a highly concentrated form of chicken stock. It's a great solution for small households because it keeps longer than leftover chicken broth.

Chicken, Bacon *and* Caramelized Onion Pasta Bake

Prep Time: 30 Minutes • Start to Finish: 50 Minutes • 2 servings

3 tablespoons butter

1 small onion, thinly sliced

1 cup uncooked penne pasta (4 oz)

2 tablespoons all-purpose flour

1½ cups milk

¼ teaspoon salt

¼ teaspoon pepper

1 cup shredded Gruyère cheese (4 oz)

¼ cup grated Parmesan cheese

1 cup shredded cooked chicken

3 slices bacon, cooked, crumbled

⅔ cup plain panko crispy bread crumbs

1 tablespoon butter, melted

1 Heat oven to 425°F. In 7-inch cast-iron or 8-inch nonstick ovenproof skillet, heat 1 tablespoon of the butter over medium heat. Add onion; cook 8 to 10 minutes, stirring occasionally, until onion is browned. Remove from heat.

2 Meanwhile, cook pasta as directed on package just until tender; drain.

3 In 2-quart saucepan, heat remaining 2 tablespoons butter over medium heat. Add flour; cook and stir 1 minute. Beat in milk, salt and pepper with whisk; heat to boiling. Reduce heat to medium-low; cook and stir 1 to 2 minutes or until thickened. Remove from heat; beat in Gruyère and Parmesan cheeses. Add cooked pasta, chicken, bacon and browned onion; gently stir to combine. Spoon into same 7-inch cast-iron skillet.

4 In small bowl, mix bread crumbs and 1 tablespoon melted butter. Sprinkle over top of pasta mixture. Bake 14 to 17 minutes or until bubbly and golden brown.

1 Serving: Calories 1230; Total Fat 62g (Saturated Fat 34g, Trans Fat 2g); Cholesterol 220mg; Sodium 1720mg; Total Carbohydrate 100g (Dietary Fiber 4g); Protein 66g **Exchanges:** 4 Starch, 2 Other Carbohydrate, ½ Milk, ½ Vegetable, 4 Lean Meat, 3 High-Fat Meat, 4 Fat **Carbohydrate Choices:** 6½

Swap It Swiss cheese can be substituted for Gruyère in this recipe.

Kitchen Tip The pasta mixture can also be baked in 8 × 4-inch loaf pan for 18 to 22 minutes.

Kitchen Tip Cook the bacon quickly by microwaving it on a microwavable plate between paper towels. Microwave on High (100%) 2 to 3 minutes. Remove paper towels; let cool.

Indian-Spiced Chicken, Cauliflower *and* Peas

Prep Time: 20 Minutes • Start to Finish: 4 Hours 30 Minutes • 2 servings (1 cup each)

2 tablespoons tomato paste

1 tablespoon water

2 teaspoons garam masala

½ teaspoon salt

1 boneless skinless chicken thigh, cut into 1-inch pieces (⅓ cup)

1 cup cubed (¾-inch) peeled sweet potato

1 plum (Roma) tomato, coarsely chopped

¼ cup coarsely chopped onion

1 cup cauliflower florets

¼ cup frozen peas, thawed

2 tablespoons plain Greek yogurt

1 tablespoon chopped cilantro

Hot cooked rice, if desired

1 In 2-quart slow cooker, stir together tomato paste, water, garam masala and salt. Stir in chicken. Layer sweet potato, tomato, onion and cauliflower over chicken.

2 Cover; cook on Low heat 4 hours or until chicken is no longer pink and vegetables are tender. Stir in peas; cover and cook 10 minutes longer or until peas are cooked.

3 Spoon mixture onto serving plates. Top each with yogurt and cilantro. Serve with rice.

1 Serving: Calories 170; Total Fat 2g (Saturated Fat 0.5g, Trans Fat 0g); Cholesterol 30mg; Sodium 700mg; Total Carbohydrate 26g (Dietary Fiber 5g); Protein 12g **Exchanges:** 1 Starch, 1½ Vegetable, 1 Very Lean Meat **Carbohydrate Choices:** 2

Kitchen Tip
Garam masala is a blend of aromatic spices used in Indian cuisine. The blend will vary among regions and even from one home to the next. Buy garam masala in the spice aisle of well-stocked grocery stores or purchase online.

Swap It
Mashed potatoes, couscous or quinoa can be substituted for the rice.

Slow-Cooker Chicken in Red Wine

Prep Time: 20 Minutes • Start to Finish: 5 Hours 50 Minutes • 4 servings

3 slices bacon

4 boneless skinless chicken thighs

1 cup ready-to-eat baby-cut carrots

½ cup frozen pearl onions

½ teaspoon salt

Dash pepper

½ teaspoon dried thyme leaves

1 clove garlic, finely chopped

1 dried bay leaf

⅔ cup dry red wine

⅓ cup chicken broth (from 32-oz carton)

1 cup small whole mushrooms

1 tablespoon all-purpose flour

1 tablespoon cold water

1 tablespoon chopped fresh parsley

1 Line microwavable plate with microwavable paper towel. Add bacon; cover with paper towel. Microwave on High 3 to 5 minutes or until crisp. Crumble bacon.

2 Spray 1½-quart slow cooker with cooking spray. Place chicken in cooker. Add carrots, onions, bacon, salt, pepper, thyme, garlic, bay leaf, wine and broth.

3 Cover; cook on High setting 4 to 5 hours.

4 Skim any fat from surface of chicken mixture. Stir in mushrooms. In small bowl, mix flour and water; stir into chicken mixture. Stir in parsley.

5 Cover; cook about 30 minutes longer or until mixture is thickened. Remove bay leaf before serving.

1 Serving: Calories 190; Total Fat 7g (Saturated Fat 2g, Trans Fat 0g); Cholesterol 100mg; Sodium 570mg; Total Carbohydrate 7g (Dietary Fiber 1g); Protein 23g **Exchanges:** 1½ Vegetable, 3 Very Lean Meat, 1 Fat **Carbohydrate Choices:** ½

Kitchen Tip This robust chicken dish, known as Coq au Vin in France, gets its wonderful flavor and rich color from the red wine and bacon. It is usually prepared with bone-in chicken pieces, but we found that boneless chicken thighs work best in the slow cooker. The chicken becomes very tender and will fall apart into pieces for easier serving.

Swap It If you prefer not to use red wine, you can still make a delicious chicken dish your family will love. Just add extra chicken broth in place of the wine.

Easy Baked Chicken *and* Potato Dinner

Prep Time: 20 Minutes • Start to Finish: 1 Hour • 2 servings

3	tablespoons olive oil
2	tablespoons Original Bisquick mix
3	tablespoons grated Parmesan cheese, if desired
1/8	teaspoon paprika
3	tablespoons Dijon mustard
1	tablespoon water
2	boneless skinless chicken breasts
4	small red potatoes, cut into quarters
1	small red or green bell pepper, thinly sliced
1	small onion, cut into 8 wedges

1 Heat oven to 400°F. Line 15 × 10 × 1-inch pan with foil. Drizzle center of pan with 1 tablespoon of olive oil.

2 In shallow dish, place Bisquick mix, 1 tablespoon Parmesan cheese and paprika. In small bowl, combine remaining 2 tablespoons olive oil, Dijon mustard and water. Brush chicken with 1 tablespoon of the mustard mixture; then coat with Bisquick mixture. Place chicken breasts on center of pan; turn to coat in olive oil.

3 In medium bowl, combine potatoes, bell pepper and onion; stir in remaining mustard mixture. Place vegetables around chicken in pan. Sprinkle evenly with remaining Parmesan cheese.

4 Bake 30 to 35 minutes until potatoes are tender and juice of chicken is clear when center of thickest part is cut (at least 165°F).

1 Serving: Calories 540; Total Fat 28g (Saturated Fat 4.5g, Trans Fat 0g); Cholesterol 100mg; Sodium 720mg; Total Carbohydrate 31g (Dietary Fiber 4g); Protein 41g **Exchanges:** 1½ Starch, 1 Vegetable, 5 Very Lean Meat, 5 Fat **Carbohydrate Choices:** 2

Swap It Try different varieties of potatoes for color and flavor. Choose Yukon Gold, purple, yellow Finnish or Texas finger potatoes.

Buffalo-Style Turkey Tenderloin

Prep Time: 25 Minutes • Start to Finish: 25 Minutes • 2 servings

1 teaspoon olive oil

1 turkey breast tenderloin (8 oz)

1 cup refrigerated cooked new potato wedges (from 20-oz bag)

1 medium onion, chopped (½ cup)

½ medium red bell pepper, chopped (½ cup)

2 tablespoons reduced-fat blue cheese dressing

1 to 3 teaspoons cayenne pepper sauce

Chopped fresh parsley, if desired

1 In 12-inch nonstick skillet, heat oil over medium-low heat. Add turkey; cover and cook 10 minutes, turning after 5 minutes.

2 Add potatoes, onion and bell pepper to turkey in skillet. Cook, uncovered, about 5 minutes longer, stirring occasionally and adding 1 to 2 tablespoons water if needed, until juice of turkey is clear when center of thickest part is cut (165°F) and potatoes are tender.

3 Meanwhile, in small bowl, mix dressing and pepper sauce. Pour sauce over turkey mixture, stirring to coat. Reduce heat to low. Cook until sauce is thoroughly heated. Sprinkle with parsley.

1 Serving: Calories 260; Total Fat 4.5g (Saturated Fat 1g, Trans Fat 0g); Cholesterol 70mg; Sodium 230mg; Total Carbohydrate 25g (Dietary Fiber 3g); Protein 29g **Exchanges:** 1 Starch, ½ Other Carbohydrate, 1 Vegetable, 3½ Very Lean Meat, ½ Fat **Carbohydrate Choices:** 1½

Kitchen Tip The heat and amount of flavor of pepper sauce vary by brand. The original cayenne pepper sauce has a sweeter flavor that is perfect for this buffalo-style entrée.

Roasted Chicken *and* Vegetables Sheet Pan Dinner

Prep Time: 15 Minutes • Start to Finish: 1 Hour • 2 servings

1 medium unpeeled russet potato, cut into 1-inch pieces

1 cup cauliflower florets

1 tablespoon butter, melted

⅛ teaspoon ground red pepper (cayenne)

1 cup large broccoli florets

2 bone-in skin-on chicken thighs

2 teaspoons Montreal chicken grill seasoning

1 tablespoon chopped fresh Italian (flat-leaf) parsley

1 Heat oven to 425°F. Spray 15 × 10 × 1-inch pan with cooking spray. In medium bowl, mix potato, cauliflower, melted butter and red pepper; pour into pan. Bake 20 minutes.

2 Stir broccoli into potato mixture in pan. Rub chicken thighs with grill seasoning. Place skin side up in pan.

3 Bake 25 to 30 minutes or until juice of chicken is clear when thickest part is cut to bone (at least 165°F) and vegetables are tender. Top with parsley.

1 Serving: Calories 290; Total Fat 11g (Saturated Fat 5g, Trans Fat 0g); Cholesterol 105mg; Sodium 400mg; Total Carbohydrate 24g (Dietary Fiber 4g); Protein 24g **Exchanges:** 1 Other Carbohydrate, 1½ Vegetable, 3 Lean Meat, ½ Fat **Carbohydrate Choices:** 1½

Kitchen Tip Look for similar-sized chicken thighs so that they cook at the same rate.

Sriracha Chicken *with* Roasted Broccoli *and* Cauliflower

Prep Time: 35 Minutes • Start to Finish: 35 Minutes • 2 servings

2 cups broccoli florets, cut into bite-size pieces

2 cups cauliflower florets, cut into bite-size pieces

2 teaspoons olive oil

⅛ teaspoon salt

2 teaspoons Sriracha sauce

2 teaspoons honey

1 teaspoon ketchup

2 boneless skinless chicken breasts (4 oz each)

⅛ teaspoon salt

4 lemon wedges

1 Center 2 oven racks in oven. Heat oven to 400°F. Line 2 (13 × 9-inch) pans with foil; spray with cooking spray. In medium bowl, toss broccoli and cauliflower with olive oil and ⅛ teaspoon salt. Place in pan on upper rack in oven.

2 Bake broccoli and cauliflower 10 minutes.

3 Meanwhile, in small bowl, mix Sriracha sauce, honey and ketchup. Place chicken breasts in other pan; rub ⅛ teaspoon salt into chicken. Stir broccoli and cauliflower; return to oven on lower rack. Place chicken on upper rack.

4 Bake both pans 10 minutes; brush Sriracha mixture on chicken, and stir vegetables. Bake 5 to 10 minutes longer or until juice of chicken is clear when center of thickest part is cut (at least 165°F) and vegetables are tender when pierced with knife.

5 Divide broccoli and cauliflower between 2 plates. Place chicken breasts on top; pour any juices over chicken. Serve with lemon wedges.

1 Serving: Calories 280; Total Fat 9g (Saturated Fat 2g, Trans Fat 0g); Cholesterol 70mg; Sodium 550mg; Total Carbohydrate 20g (Dietary Fiber 5g); Protein 30g **Exchanges:** ½ Other Carbohydrate, 2½ Vegetable, 3½ Very Lean Meat, 1½ Fat **Carbohydrate Choices:** 1

Swap It Don't have Sriracha? Try adding chili-garlic sauce instead.

BEEF
and
PORK

One-Pot Meatball Stroganoff

Prep Time: 15 Minutes • Start to Finish: 30 Minutes • 2 servings

2 tablespoons butter

4 oz sliced baby bella or cremini mushrooms (about 1⅓ cups)

⅛ teaspoon salt

⅛ teaspoon pepper

2 cups beef broth (from 32-oz carton)

2 cups uncooked wide egg noodles

12 frozen fully cooked beef meatballs, thawed (from 22-oz bag)

⅓ cup sour cream

1 In 2-quart saucepan, heat butter over medium-high heat. Add mushrooms, salt and pepper; cook 3 to 5 minutes, stirring frequently, until tender.

2 Add beef broth, egg noodles and meatballs; heat to boiling. Reduce heat to medium; simmer 9 to 11 minutes, stirring occasionally, until liquid is mostly absorbed. Remove from heat; let stand 5 minutes.

3 Stir in sour cream; serve immediately.

1 Serving: Calories 760; Total Fat 42g (Saturated Fat 20g, Trans Fat 1.5g); Cholesterol 250mg; Sodium 2040mg; Total Carbohydrate 52g (Dietary Fiber 3g); Protein 42g **Exchanges:** 2½ Starch, ½ Other Carbohydrate, 1½ Vegetable, 4½ Lean Meat, 5½ Fat **Carbohydrate Choices:** 3½

Swap It White button mushrooms may be substituted for baby bella mushrooms.

Easy Beef Enchiladas

Prep Time: 20 Minutes • Start to Finish: 1 Hour • 2 servings

½ lb lean (at least 80%) ground beef

1 can (10 oz) mild enchilada sauce

¾ cup black bean and corn salsa (from 16-oz jar)

1 cup shredded Mexican four-cheese blend (4 oz)

4 flour tortillas for burritos (8 inch)

Chopped fresh cilantro, if desired

1 Heat oven to 350°F. Spray 8-inch square (2-quart) glass baking dish with cooking spray.

2 In 10-inch skillet, cook ground beef over medium-high heat 5 to 7 minutes, stirring frequently, until no longer pink; drain. In medium bowl, mix cooked beef, ¼ cup of the enchilada sauce, the salsa and ½ cup of the cheese.

3 Divide beef mixture evenly (about ½ cup each) among tortillas. Wrap tortillas around filling; place seam side down in baking dish.

4 Pour remaining enchilada sauce over tortillas, and top with remaining ½ cup cheese. Cover baking dish with foil. Bake 35 to 40 minutes or until thoroughly heated. Sprinkle with cilantro.

1 Serving: Calories 730; Total Fat 37g (Saturated Fat 18g, Trans Fat 3g); Cholesterol 125mg; Sodium 1880mg; Total Carbohydrate 59g (Dietary Fiber 3g); Protein 40g **Exchanges:** 3 Starch, 1 Other Carbohydrate, 2½ Lean Meat, 2 High-Fat Meat, 2½ Fat **Carbohydrate Choices:** 4

Kitchen Tip Serve the enchiladas with shredded lettuce, guacamole, salsa, sour cream and chopped fresh cilantro.

Swap It Use spicy enchilada sauce if you prefer more heat.

Barbecued Beef *and* Veggie Packets

Prep Time: 30 Minutes • Start to Finish: 30 Minutes • 4 servings

4 medium potatoes, thinly sliced (4 cups)

8 large mushrooms, sliced (2 cups)

4 large carrots, thinly sliced (2 cups)

2 medium onions, sliced

½ lb extra-lean (at least 90%) ground beef

1 cup barbecue sauce

1 Heat oven to 450°F. Cut 4 (20 × 18-inch) sheets of heavy-duty foil. Fold each in half to form 10 × 18-inch rectangle.

2 In large bowl, mix potatoes, mushrooms, carrots and onions. Crumble beef over vegetables. Add barbecue sauce; toss until well coated. Spoon one-fourth of mixture onto each sheet of foil. Bring up 2 sides of foil so edges meet. Seal edges, making tight ½-inch fold; fold again, allowing space for heat circulation and expansion. Fold other sides to seal. Repeat with 3 other sheets of foil. Place packets on cookie sheet.

3 Bake packets, turning over once, 15 to 20 minutes until beef is thoroughly cooked and veggies are crisp-tender. Carefully open packets to allow steam to escape.

1 Serving: Calories 370; Total Fat 5g (Saturated Fat 2g, Trans Fat 0g); Cholesterol 35mg; Sodium 740mg; Total Carbohydrate 65g (Dietary Fiber 7g); Protein 16g **Exchanges:** 2 Starch, 1½ Other Carbohydrate, 2 Vegetable, 1 Lean Meat **Carbohydrate Choices:** 4

Grilled BBQ Beef and Veggie Packets

Prepare as directed except heat gas or charcoal grill. Place packets on grill over medium heat. Cover grill; cook 20 minutes, turning packets over once, until beef is thoroughly cooked and veggies are crisp-tender.

Beef Fajitas

Prep Time: 20 Minutes • Start to Finish: 20 Minutes • 2 servings (2 fajitas each)

½ lb boneless beef sirloin steak (½ to ¾ inch thick)

1 teaspoon vegetable oil

4 teaspoons taco seasoning mix (from 1-oz package)

2 cups frozen bell pepper and onion stir-fry (from 1-lb bag), thawed, well drained

4 flour tortillas for soft tacos and fajitas (6 inch), heated

½ cup chunky-style salsa

1 Heat closed contact grill 5 minutes. Brush both sides of steak with oil; rub with 2 teaspoons of the taco seasoning mix. Sprinkle vegetables with remaining taco seasoning mix.

2 When grill is heated, place steak and vegetables on bottom grill surface. Close grill; cook 4 to 8 minutes or until desired beef doneness.

3 Slice steak diagonally across grain into thin slices. Wrap steak and vegetables in warm tortillas; top with salsa.

1 Serving: Calories 420; Total Fat 11g (Saturated Fat 2.5g, Trans Fat 1.5g); Cholesterol 65mg; Sodium 1430mg; Total Carbohydrate 49g (Dietary Fiber 3g); Protein 32g **Exchanges:** 2½ Starch, ½ Other Carbohydrate, 1 Vegetable, 3 Lean Meat **Carbohydrate Choices:** 3

Kitchen Tip If you like your meat well done, add the vegetables after the steaks have cooked for 2 minutes. The veggies will overcook if you add them any earlier.

Black *and* Blue Mini Meat Loaves

Prep Time: 10 Minutes • Start to Finish: 50 Minutes • 2 loaves

LOAVES

- ½ lb lean (at least 80%) ground beef
- ⅓ cup plain panko crispy bread crumbs
- ¼ cup crumbled blue cheese (1 oz)
- 2 tablespoons sliced green onions (2 medium)
- 1 tablespoon chopped fresh Italian (flat-leaf) parsley
- 1 tablespoon milk
- 2 teaspoons Dijon mustard
- ½ teaspoon seasoned pepper
- 1 egg

TOPPINGS

Crumbled blue cheese, if desired

Sliced green onions, if desired

1 Heat oven to 350°F. In medium bowl, mix all ingredients except toppings. Shape mixture into 2 small (4 × 2-inch) loaves. Place in 2 ungreased 4½ × 2½-inch loaf pans.

2 Bake, uncovered, 30 to 35 minutes or until meat thermometer inserted in center of loaves reads 160°F.

3 Let stand 5 minutes; remove from pans. Garnish with toppings.

1 Loaf: Calories 370; Total Fat 21g (Saturated Fat 9g, Trans Fat 0.5g); Cholesterol 175mg; Sodium 520mg; Total Carbohydrate 15g (Dietary Fiber 0g); Protein 29g **Exchanges:** 1 Starch, 2½ Lean Meat, 1 High-Fat Meat, 1 Fat **Carbohydrate Choices:** 1

Swap It For a different flavor, substitute feta cheese for the blue cheese and ½ teaspoon dried oregano for the parsley.

Kitchen Tip If you don't have mini loaf pans, use 2 (10-ounce) custard cups and shape the meat mixture into two round loaves. Bake as directed.

Teriyaki Beef–Stuffed Peppers

Prep Time: 25 Minutes • Start to Finish: 1 Hour 10 Minutes • 2 servings

½   cup uncooked instant white rice

½   cup beef broth (from 32-oz carton)

2   large red bell peppers

½   lb lean (at least 80%) ground beef

2   green onions, thinly sliced on the bias, white and green parts separated

½   cup shredded carrots

3   tablespoons packed brown sugar

2   tablespoons soy sauce

1   tablespoon chile garlic sauce

½   teaspoon ground ginger

½   cup shredded mozzarella cheese (2 oz)

1 Heat oven to 425°F. Spray 8-inch square (2-quart) glass baking dish with cooking spray. In medium bowl, mix rice and broth. Cut each bell pepper in half vertically. Remove seeds and membranes; place cut side up in baking dish.

2 In 10-inch nonstick skillet, cook beef, green onion whites and shredded carrots over medium heat 8 to 9 minutes, stirring occasionally, until beef is deep brown and vegetables soften. Stir in brown sugar, soy sauce, chile garlic sauce and ginger; cook 1 to 2 minutes longer or until sauce is absorbed. Stir beef mixture into rice mixture. Stir in cheese.

3 Divide beef mixture evenly among bell peppers in baking dish. Cover tightly with foil.

4 Bake 45 to 50 minutes or until bell peppers and rice are tender; top with green onion greens.

1 Serving: Calories 620; Total Fat 19g (Saturated Fat 8g, Trans Fat 1g); Cholesterol 85mg; Sodium 1560mg; Total Carbohydrate 78g (Dietary Fiber 5g); Protein 34g **Exchanges:** 2 Starch, 2½ Other Carbohydrate, 2 Vegetable, 3 Very Lean Meat, ½ Medium-Fat Meat, 3 Fat **Carbohydrate Choices:** 5

Swap It An easy flavor switch is to use ground turkey instead of the ground beef.

Ancho Chili Beef Soup

Prep Time: 15 Minutes • Start to Finish: 35 Minutes • 3 servings (1⅓ cups each)

SOUP

- ¼ lb lean (at least 80%) ground beef
- ⅓ cup chopped onion
- 2 cups water
- 2 teaspoons roasted beef base (from 8-oz jar)
- 1 can (10 oz) diced tomatoes and green chiles
- ½ cup black beans, rinsed, drained (from 15-oz can)
- ½ cup whole kernel corn with red and green peppers, undrained (from 11-oz can)
- 1 teaspoon ground ancho chile pepper
- ½ teaspoon garlic powder
- ½ teaspoon ground cumin

TOPPINGS

- Chopped fresh cilantro, if desired
- Shredded Cheddar cheese, if desired

1 In 2-quart saucepan, cook ground beef and onion over medium heat 4 to 6 minutes, or until beef is thoroughly cooked.

2 Stir in remaining soup ingredients. Heat to boiling; reduce heat to low. Cover; simmer 20 minutes, stirring occasionally.

3 Ladle soup into bowls; sprinkle with cilantro and cheese.

1 Serving: Calories 180; Total Fat 6g (Saturated Fat 2g, Trans Fat 0g); Cholesterol 25mg; Sodium 1440mg; Total Carbohydrate 21g (Dietary Fiber 5g); Protein 10g **Exchanges:** 1 Starch, 1 Vegetable, 1 Lean Meat, ½ Fat **Carbohydrate Choices:** 1½

Swap It Try swapping lean ground turkey for ground beef in this soup.

Use It Up Use the leftover canned ingredients to make a quick topping for nachos.

Kitchen Tip Beef base is a concentrated paste that should be refrigerated after opening. It is a handy staple to use instead of a can or carton of beef broth.

Slow-Cooker Cowboy Stew

Prep Time: 10 Minutes • Start to Finish: 10 Hours 10 Minutes • 2 servings

6   oz beef stew meat, cut into ½-inch pieces

1   potato, unpeeled, cut into 1-inch pieces

¼   cup chopped onion

¼   teaspoon salt

⅛   teaspoon pepper

1   can (16 oz) baked beans in barbecue sauce

1 In 2½- to 3½-quart slow cooker, mix beef, potato, onion, salt and pepper. Spread beans over beef mixture.

2 Cover and cook on Low heat setting 8 to 10 hours or until beef is tender.

1 Serving: Calories 530; Total Fat 9g (Saturated Fat 3.5g, Trans Fat 0g); Cholesterol 45mg; Sodium 1340mg; Total Carbohydrate 84g (Dietary Fiber 15g); Protein 29g **Exchanges:** 3½ Starch, 2 Other Carbohydrate, 2½ Very Lean Meat, 1 Fat **Carbohydrate Choices:** 5½

Philly Cheesesteak Casserole

Prep Time: 25 Minutes • Start to Finish: 1 Hour 10 Minutes • 2 servings (1½ cups each)

1½ cups uncooked dumpling or wide egg noodles (3 oz)

½ lb boneless beef sirloin steak, about ¾ inch thick

¼ teaspoon pepper

1 medium onion, chopped (½ cup)

½ small green bell pepper, chopped (¼ cup)

¾ cup beef broth (from 32-oz carton)

2 tablespoons all-purpose flour

¼ cup fat-free half-and-half

2 teaspoons Dijon mustard

⅓ cup shredded reduced-fat Cheddar cheese (1 oz)

1 Heat oven to 350°F. Spray 8-inch square (2-quart) glass baking dish with cooking spray. Cook and drain noodles as directed on package.

2 Meanwhile, remove fat from beef. Cut beef into ¾-inch pieces. Heat 10-inch nonstick skillet over medium heat. Cook beef and pepper in skillet 2 to 3 minutes, stirring occasionally, until beef is brown. Stir in onion and bell pepper. Cook 2 minutes, stirring occasionally. Spoon into baking dish.

3 In medium bowl, beat broth and flour with whisk until smooth. Add to skillet; heat to boiling. Cook, stirring constantly, until mixture thickens; remove from heat. Stir in half-and-half and mustard. Spoon over beef mixture. Stir in cooked noodles.

4 Cover and bake 40 minutes. Sprinkle with cheese. Bake, uncovered, about 5 minutes longer or until cheese is melted and casserole is bubbly.

1 Serving: Calories 390; Total Fat 10g (Saturated Fat 4.5g, Trans Fat 0g); Cholesterol 105mg; Sodium 800mg: Total Carbohydrate 37g (Dietary Fiber 2g); Protein 37g **Exchanges:** 1½ Starch, ½ Other Carbohydrate, 1 Vegetable, 4 Very Lean Meat, ½ High-Fat Meat, ½ Fat **Carbohydrate Choices:** 2½

Kitchen Tip To test pasta for doneness, run a piece under cold water, then bite into it. It's done if still slightly firm.

Kitchen Tip Spraying the baking dish with cooking spray allows the food to release easily and makes cleanup a snap.

Beef *and* Vegetable Stir-Fry

Prep Time: 15 Minutes • Start to Finish: 15 Minutes • 2 servings

1 cup uncooked instant white rice

1 cup water

¼ lb extra-lean (at least 90%) ground beef

1 small onion, sliced

1½ cups frozen broccoli florets, thawed

½ red bell pepper, cut into thin bite-size strips

2 tablespoons stir-fry sauce

2 tablespoons water

½ teaspoon grated gingerroot

1 Cook rice in 1 cup water as directed on package.

2 Meanwhile, in medium nonstick skillet, cook ground beef and onion over medium heat until beef is thoroughly cooked, stirring frequently. Drain.

3 Add all remaining ingredients; cover and cook 4 to 6 minutes or until vegetables are crisp-tender, stirring occasionally. Serve vegetable mixture over rice.

1 Serving: Calories 350; Total Fat 6g (Saturated Fat 2g, Trans Fat 0g); Cholesterol 35mg; Sodium 1200mg; Total Carbohydrate 58g (Dietary Fiber 4g); Protein 17g **Exchanges:** 2 Starch, 1½ Other Carbohydrate, 1½ Vegetable, 1 Very Lean Meat, 1 Fat **Carbohydrate Choices:** 4

Kitchen Tip For small amounts of vegetables, such as the bell pepper in this recipe, stop at the salad bar and purchase just the amount you need.

Curried Beef Pizzas

Prep Time: 35 Minutes • Start to Finish: 2 Hours 55 Minutes • 2 servings

CRUST

1	package regular or fast-acting dry yeast (2¼ teaspoons)
½	cup warm water (105°F to 115°F)
1¼ to 1½	cups all-purpose flour
1	teaspoon olive or vegetable oil
½	teaspoon salt
½	teaspoon sugar

TOPPINGS

½	lb lean (at least 80%) ground beef
1	cup diced zucchini
1	teaspoon curry powder
1	teaspoon finely chopped garlic
	Dash salt
2	tablespoons chutney
¼	cup sour cream
1	cup shredded mozzarella cheese (4 oz)
1	thin slice red onion, separated into rings
¼	cup chopped tomato
¼	cup crumbled feta cheese

1 In large bowl, dissolve yeast in warm water. With wooden spoon, stir in ¾ cup of the flour, the oil, ½ teaspoon salt and sugar. Stir in enough of the remaining flour, ¼ cup at a time, until dough is easy to handle.

2 Place dough on lightly floured surface. Knead 5 to 7 minutes or until dough is smooth and elastic. Spray large bowl with cooking spray. Place dough in bowl, turning dough to grease all sides. Cover bowl loosely with plastic wrap; let rise in warm place 20 minutes or until dough is increased in size by 1½ times.

3 Gently push fist into dough to deflate. Cover bowl loosely with plastic wrap; refrigerate at least 2 hours but no longer than 48 hours. (If dough should double in size during refrigeration, gently push fist into dough to deflate it.)

4 Move oven rack to lowest position in oven. Heat oven to 425°F. In 10-inch nonstick skillet, cook ground beef over medium-high heat 4 to 5 minutes, stirring occasionally, until beef is thoroughly cooked. Stir in zucchini and ½ teaspoon of the curry powder; cook, stirring constantly, until zucchini is tender, about 4 minutes. Add garlic; cook 1 minute. Remove from heat; stir in salt and chutney.

5 Divide dough for crust in half and shape each into ball. Place dough balls on opposite corners of ungreased large cookie sheet. Press each into an 8-inch round. Press dough from center to edge so the edges are slightly thicker than the center. Crusts should be about 1½ inches apart on cookie sheet.

6 In small bowl, combine sour cream and remaining ½ teaspoon curry powder. Spread sour cream mixture over each dough round to within ½ inch of edge. Top each with ½ cup of the mozzarella cheese. Spoon the ground beef mixture evenly over mozzarella cheese on pizzas. Top with sliced red onion rings, tomato and feta cheese.

7 Bake 15 to 20 minutes or until crust is golden brown.

1 Serving: Calories 840; Total Fat 37g (Saturated Fat 17g, Trans Fat 1.5g); Cholesterol 140mg; Sodium 1400mg; Total Carbohydrate 78g (Dietary Fiber 5g); Protein 47g **Exchanges:** 5 Starch, 1 Vegetable, 4 Lean Meat, 4½ Fat **Carbohydrate Choices:** 5

Swap It Use 8-inch flatbread in place of the scratch pizza dough. Top the flatbread as directed in the recipe, and then bake just until the cheese is melted and the topping is heated through.

Beef *and* Vegetable–Topped Potato Halves

Prep Time: 25 Minutes • Start to Finish: 25 Minutes • 2 servings

1   medium baking potato

1   teaspoon olive or vegetable oil

4   oz beef flank steak, cut across grain into thin bite-size strips

1   cup sliced fresh mushrooms

1   small onion, cut into thin wedges

½   teaspoon garlic powder

⅛   teaspoon pepper

1   can (18.5 oz) light savory vegetable barley soup

¼   cup fat-free sour cream

2   tablespoons chopped fresh parsley

1 Generously pierce potato with fork; place on microwavable paper towel. Microwave on High 4 to 5 minutes, turning once, until tender. Cover; let stand covered 5 minutes.

2 Meanwhile, in 12-inch nonstick skillet, heat oil over high heat. Add beef, mushrooms and onion; sprinkle with garlic powder and pepper. Cook 5 to 7 minutes, stirring frequently, just until beef is browned and vegetables are just tender.

3 Stir in soup. Heat to boiling. Cook, uncovered, over high heat 7 to 10 minutes, stirring frequently, until mixture thickens. Remove from heat; stir in sour cream.

4 To serve, place ½ potato on each serving plate. Top each with 1½ cups beef mixture; sprinkle each with 1 tablespoon parsley.

1 Serving: Calories 300; Total Fat 4.5g (Saturated Fat 1g, Trans Fat 0g); Cholesterol 40mg; Sodium 830mg; Total Carbohydrate 43g (Dietary Fiber 7g); Protein 20g **Exchanges:** 1 Starch, 1½ Other Carbohydrate, 1½ Vegetable, 2 Very Lean Meat, ½ Fat **Carbohydrate Choices:** 3

Kitchen Tip
Freeze the beef for 15 to 20 minutes, and it will be easier to cut.

Swap It
Boneless beef sirloin is an ideal substitute for the flank steak.

BEEF AND PORK   95

Slow-Cooker Beef Stroganoff

Prep Time: 10 Minutes • Start to Finish: 10 Hours 10 Minutes • 2 servings

½ lb beef stew meat, cut into ½-inch pieces

¼ cup chopped onion

1 can (10¾ oz) condensed golden mushroom soup

1 jar (2½ oz) sliced mushrooms, drained

⅛ teaspoon pepper

½ cup sour cream

1½ cups hot cooked noodles or rice

Additional pepper, if desired

1 In 2½- to 3½-quart slow cooker, mix beef, onion, soup, mushrooms and pepper.

2 Cover and cook on Low heat setting 8 to 10 hours or until beef is very tender.

3 Stir sour cream into beef mixture. Serve over noodles. Sprinkle with additional pepper.

1 Serving: Calories 610; Total Fat 32g (Saturated Fat 12g, Trans Fat 1g); Cholesterol 100mg; Sodium 1250mg; Total Carbohydrate 49g (Dietary Fiber 4g); Protein 31g **Exchanges:** 2 Starch, 1 Other Carbohydrate, ½ Vegetable, 3½ Lean Meat, 4 Fat **Carbohydrate Choices:** 3

Kitchen Tip If purchasing small quantities of beef is not possible, buy the regular quantity, then divide and freeze for later use.

Cook Once, Eat Twice

Cook these recipes for dinner, then use the remaining portions later in the week for another meal in a snap! Prepare second meal within 3 to 4 days of making the first meal.

FIRST DINNER	SECOND DINNER
Chicken Waldorf Salad (page 32) Prepare as directed except reserve 2 lettuce leaves and half the salad and chives; cover and refrigerate.	**Crunchy Chicken Cashew Wraps** Toss reserved salad with the chives and ½ cup cashew pieces. Spoon mixture evenly onto four 7 or 8-inch flour tortillas. Top each with ½ lettuce leaf. Roll up each tortilla.
Gluten-Free Buffalo Chicken Salad (page 35) Prepare as directed except reserve half of the cooked chicken, the dressing (in step 4) and salad ingredients. Cover and refrigerate.	**Buffalo Chicken Taco Salad** Reheat chicken, if desired. Toss reserved salad ingredients with dressing. Toss with chicken. Spread ½ to 1 cup of gluten-free corn or tortilla chips onto dinner plates; top with salad mixture.
Slow-Cooker Chicken in Red Wine (page 64) Prepare as directed except reserve half of the cooked mixture in a microwavable bowl; cover with plastic wrap and refrigerate.	**Savory Chicken-Topped Potatoes** Turn back one corner of plastic wrap on bowl. Microwave on Medium (50%) about 2 minutes or until heated through. Serve over hot mashed potatoes.
Barbecued Beef and Veggie Packets (page 80) Prepare as directed except reserve 2 packets. When packets are cool, rewrap in the foil and refrigerate.	**Scrambled Eggs with Barbecue Beef-Veggie Hash** Chop veggies from reserved packets into bite-size pieces; heat mixture in skillet before adding eggs to make scrambled eggs.
Grilled Southwestern Pork Chops (see photo on right) Prepare as directed except reserve 2 pork chops; wrap and refrigerate.	**Southwestern Pork Burrito Bowls** (see photo on right) Cut pork chops into bite-size pieces; reheat, if desired. Spoon hot quinoa or rice into serving bowls. Spoon pork pieces on top of quinoa. Top with ¾ cup pico de gallo, cubed fresh avocado, hot cooked corn and black beans. Top with shredded Colby–Monterey Jack cheese blend.

Hungarian Beef Goulash *with* Sour Cream Dumplings

Prep Time: 30 Minutes • Start to Finish: 40 Minutes • 2 servings

GOULASH

- 1 tablespoon olive oil
- 12 oz top sirloin steak, cut into 1-inch cubes
- ½ teaspoon salt
- ½ teaspoon pepper
- 2 slices bacon, chopped
- ½ cup chopped onion
- ¾ cup chopped red bell pepper
- 1 tablespoon tomato paste
- 1 clove garlic, finely chopped
- 1 tablespoon paprika
- 1½ cups beef broth (from 32-oz carton)

DUMPLINGS

- ⅔ cup Original Bisquick mix
- ⅓ cup sour cream
- 2 tablespoons milk
- 1 tablespoon chives

- ¼ cup sour cream

1 In 10-inch skillet, heat oil over medium-high heat. Sprinkle steak with salt and pepper; add to skillet. Cook 2 to 3 minutes, turning steak cubes, until brown on all sides. Transfer to plate; reduce heat to medium.

2 Add bacon to skillet; cook and stir 2 to 3 minutes, until just beginning to brown. Add onion, bell pepper, tomato paste and garlic; cook about 5 minutes, stirring occasionally, until vegetables are just tender. Add paprika; cook about 1 minute or until fragrant. Add broth; reduce heat to medium. Cook 5 minutes.

3 Meanwhile, in small bowl, stir Bisquick mix, ⅓ cup sour cream, the milk and chives.

4 Add browned beef to goulash. Drop dumpling dough in 6 generous tablespoonfuls on top. Reduce heat to medium-low; cover. Cook 8 to 10 minutes or until dumplings are cooked through. Serve with ¼ cup sour cream on the side.

1 Serving: Calories 800; Total Fat 41g (Saturated Fat 16g, Trans Fat 0.5g); Cholesterol 140mg; Sodium 1990mg; Total Carbohydrate 57g (Dietary Fiber 11g); Protein 50g **Exchanges:** 1 Starch, 2½ Other Carbohydrate, 1 Vegetable, 6½ Lean Meat, 4 Fat **Carbohydrate Choices:** 4

Barbecued Beef Shepherd's Pie

Prep Time: 15 Minutes • Start to Finish: 1 Hour 10 Minutes • 2 servings (1¼ cups each)

¾ cup barbecue sauce with shredded beef (from 16-oz container)

½ cup frozen whole kernel corn, thawed

¼ cup chopped fresh tomato

¼ cup sliced green onions (4 medium)

2 tablespoons chopped green chiles (from 4-oz can)

1 cup refrigerated mashed potatoes

½ cup shredded Cheddar cheese

1 Heat oven to 350°F. Spray 1-quart casserole dish with cooking spray. In medium bowl, stir together beef, corn, tomato, 2 tablespoons of the green onions and 1 tablespoon of the chiles; spoon into casserole.

2 In another medium bowl, stir together potatoes, cheese, and the remaining green onions and green chiles. Spread potato mixture over beef.

3 Bake 40 to 50 minutes or until bubbling around edges and center reaches 165°F. Let stand 5 minutes before serving.

1 Serving: Calories 440; Total Fat 23g (Saturated Fat 12g, Trans Fat 1g); Cholesterol 80mg; Sodium 800mg; Total Carbohydrate 36g (Dietary Fiber 3g); Protein 22g **Exchanges:** 1½ Starch, ½ Other Carbohydrate, ½ Vegetable, 1½ Lean Meat, 1 High-Fat Meat, 2 Fat **Carbohydrate Choices:** 2½

Swap It Barbecued pulled pork or chicken can be substituted for the beef, and bite-size cooked mixed vegetables can be substituted for the corn. For more spice, try jalapeño chiles in place of the green chiles.

Use It Up Enjoy extra barbecued beef heated and spooned into pitas with red onion, diced tomatoes and shredded lettuce.

Grilled Bourbon-Glazed Beef Kabobs

Prep Time: 25 Minutes • Start to Finish: 25 Minutes • 2 servings

GLAZE

- 2 tablespoons bourbon or water
- 1 tablespoon teriyaki baste and glaze (from 12-oz bottle)
- 1 tablespoon frozen (thawed) orange juice concentrate
- ¼ cup packed brown sugar
- Dash of crushed red pepper flakes

KABOBS

- ½ lb boneless beef top sirloin, cut into 1½-inch cubes
- 8 pieces (1½-inch) red onion
- 8 large whole mushrooms
- 8 pieces (1½-inch) red bell pepper
- 1 teaspoon olive or vegetable oil
- ¼ teaspoon salt

1 Heat gas or charcoal grill. In 1-quart saucepan, mix 1 tablespoon of the bourbon, the teriyaki glaze, orange juice concentrate, brown sugar and crushed red pepper. Heat to boiling over medium heat; reduce heat to low. Simmer 5 minutes, stirring occasionally; remove from heat. Stir in remaining 1 tablespoon bourbon. Reserve 2 tablespoons glaze.

2 In medium bowl, place beef, onion, mushrooms and bell pepper. Drizzle with oil; toss to coat. Sprinkle with salt; toss to coat. On each of four 7- to 12-inch wooden skewers, thread beef, onion, mushrooms and bell pepper alternately, leaving ¼-inch space between each piece.

3 Cover and grill kabobs over medium heat 9 to 11 minutes, turning once and brushing with glaze during last 3 minutes, until beef is desired doneness and vegetables are tender.

4 Just before serving, generously brush kabobs with reserved 2 tablespoons glaze.

1 Serving: Calories 360; Total Fat 6g (Saturated Fat 1.5g, Trans Fat 0g); Cholesterol 65mg; Sodium 770mg; Total Carbohydrate 43g (Dietary Fiber 2g); Protein 28g **Carbohydrate Choices:** 3

Swap It Add more color to these kabobs by using a variety of colored bell peppers, including red, green, yellow or orange.

Kitchen Tip The perfect accompaniment for these kabobs is hot cooked rice.

Italian Beef Kabobs

Prep Time: 15 Minutes • Start to Finish: 1 Hour 25 Minutes • 2 servings

2 garlic cloves, finely chopped

¼ cup balsamic vinegar

¼ cup water

1 tablespoon chopped fresh oregano leaves or 1 teaspoon dried oregano leaves

2 tablespoons olive or vegetable oil

1½ teaspoons chopped fresh marjoram leaves or ½ teaspoon dried marjoram leaves

1 teaspoon sugar

½ lb boneless beef sirloin steak, cut into 1-inch pieces

1 Mix all ingredients except beef in medium glass or plastic bowl. Stir in beef until coated. Cover and refrigerate, stirring occasionally, at least 1 hour but no longer than 12 hours.

2 Set oven control to broil. Remove beef from marinade; reserve marinade. Thread beef on each of four 10-inch metal skewers, leaving ½-inch space between each piece. Brush kabobs with marinade.

3 Place kabobs on rack in broiler pan. Broil kabobs with tops about 3 inches from heat 6 to 8 minutes for medium-rare to medium doneness, turning and brushing with marinade after 3 minutes. Discard any remaining marinade.

1 Serving: Calories 290; Total Fat 17g (Saturated Fat 3g, Trans Fat 0g); Cholesterol 65mg; Sodium 65mg; Total Carbohydrate 9g (Dietary Fiber 0g); Protein 25g **Exchanges:** ½ Other Carbohydrate, 3½ Lean Meat, 1½ Fat **Carbohydrate Choices:** ½

Swap It To speed up prep, omit the garlic, vinegar, water, oregano, oil, marjoram and sugar, and instead marinate the beef in ⅔ cup purchased Italian dressing in step 2.

Kitchen Tip If using bamboo skewers, soak in water at least 30 minutes before using to prevent burning.

Chili-Ranch Grilled Pork

Prep Time: 25 Minutes • Start to Finish: 40 Minutes • 2 servings

2 boneless pork loin chops, ¾ inch thick (about ½ lb)

2 tablespoons reduced-fat ranch dressing

¼ teaspoon salt

¼ teaspoon chili powder

⅛ teaspoon dried thyme leaves

⅛ teaspoon garlic powder

1 Heat gas or charcoal grill. Place pork chops in shallow bowl. Pour dressing over both sides of pork chops. Cover; refrigerate 15 minutes to marinate.

2 Meanwhile, in small bowl, mix remaining ingredients. Remove pork from marinade; discard marinade.

3 Sprinkle half of seasoning mixture over one side of pork chops. Place pork on grill, seasoned side down. Sprinkle remaining seasoning mixture over pork. Cover grill; cook over medium heat 8 to 10 minutes, turning once, or until meat thermometer inserted in center reads 145°F. Let stand 3 minutes before serving.

1 Serving: Calories 210; Total Fat 11g (Saturated Fat 3g, Trans Fat 0g); Cholesterol 75mg; Sodium 480mg; Total Carbohydrate 3g (Dietary Fiber 0g); Protein 24g **Exchanges:** 3½ Very Lean Meat, 2 Fat **Carbohydrate Choices:** 0

Swap It Try this recipe using boneless skinless chicken breasts. Grill 15 to 20 minutes or until the juice of the chicken is clear when center of thickest part is cut (at least 165°F).

French Dip Sandwiches

Prep Time: 10 Minutes • Start to Finish: 10 Minutes • 2 sandwiches

1   cup French onion soup (from 18.5-oz can)

6   oz thinly sliced deli roast beef, cut into thirds

2   French rolls, cut in half horizontally

1 In 2-quart saucepan, heat soup to boiling. Reduce heat; simmer 2 minutes, stirring occasionally. Add beef; cook 2 to 3 minutes, stirring occasionally, until hot.

2 With slotted spoon, place beef and onions on bottom half of rolls. Cover with top half of rolls. Cut each sandwich in half. Serve sandwiches with remaining warm soup for dipping.

1 Sandwich: Calories 250; Total Fat 4g (Saturated Fat 1.5g, Trans Fat 0g); Cholesterol 45mg; Sodium 1590mg; Total Carbohydrate 31g (Dietary Fiber 1g); Protein 22g **Exchanges:** 2 Starch, 2 Very Lean Meat, ½ Lean Meat **Carbohydrate Choices:** 2

Swap It Spice up the sandwich with a flavorful mustard or fruity chutney.

Cajun Pot Roast *with* Maque Choux

Prep Time: 15 Minutes • Start to Finish: 8 Hours 20 Minutes • 3 servings

1 to 1½ lb boneless beef chuck roast

2 teaspoons Cajun seasoning

1 cup frozen whole kernel corn

¼ cup chopped onion

¼ cup chopped green bell pepper

1 can (14.5 oz) diced tomatoes, undrained

Dash pepper

¼ teaspoon red pepper sauce

1 Rub entire surface of beef roast with Cajun seasoning. Place roast in 3- to 3½-quart slow cooker. Top with frozen corn, onion and bell pepper.

2 In small bowl, mix tomatoes, pepper and pepper sauce. Pour over vegetables and roast.

3 Cover; cook on Low heat setting 7 to 8 hours.

4 To serve, cut roast into slices. Using a slotted spoon, remove corn mixture and serve with roast.

1 Serving: Calories 470; Total Fat 24g (Saturated Fat 9g, Trans Fat 1g); Cholesterol 125mg; Sodium 1160mg; Total Carbohydrate 18g (Dietary Fiber 3g); Protein 44g **Exchanges:** ½ Starch, ½ Other Carbohydrate, 1 Vegetable, 6 Lean Meat, 1 Fat **Carbohydrate Choices:** 1

Kitchen Tip Maque choux (pronounced MOCK shoo) means "smothered corn" in Cajun country. This corn is smothered with tomatoes, bell pepper and onion.

Slow-Cooker Cuban Flank Steak

Prep Time: 15 Minutes • Start to Finish: 8 Hours 20 Minutes • 2 servings

1   small onion, thinly sliced

½   small red bell pepper, cut into strips (½ cup)

½   small green bell pepper, cut into strips (½ cup)

½   lb beef flank steak, cut into 2 pieces

2   teaspoons chili powder

¼   teaspoon dried oregano leaves

½   teaspoon dried minced garlic

¼   teaspoon salt

2   teaspoons lime juice

¼   cup beef broth (from 32-oz carton)

½   cup uncooked regular long-grain white rice

½   cup black beans (from 15-oz can), drained, rinsed

1 Spray 1½- to 2-quart slow cooker with cooking spray. Place onion and peppers in cooker. Top with beef. Sprinkle with chili powder, oregano, garlic and salt. Drizzle with lime juice. Add broth.

2 Cover; cook on Low heat setting 6 to 8 hours.

3 About 20 minutes before serving, cook rice as directed on package.

4 Remove beef from cooker; place on cutting board. Shred beef with 2 forks; return to cooker and mix well. Stir in black beans. Increase heat setting to High. Cover; cook about 5 minutes longer or until thoroughly heated. Serve beef and sauce over rice.

1 Serving: Calories 460; Total Fat 6g (Saturated Fat 2g, Trans Fat 0g); Cholesterol 85mg; Sodium 470mg; Total Carbohydrate 60g (Dietary Fiber 7g); Protein 42g **Exchanges:** 3½ Starch, 1 Vegetable, 4 Very Lean Meat, ½ Fat **Carbohydrate Choices:** 4

Kitchen Tip The sauce that collects is packed with flavor, but if you prefer, drain excess sauce before serving.

Use It Up The remaining black beans can be rinsed and drained, and then used in any salad or for another main dish.

Filet Mignon *with* Creamy Blue Cheese Sauce

Prep Time: 35 Minutes • Start to Finish: 35 Minutes • 2 servings

2 boneless beef tenderloin steaks, 1½ inches thick

½ teaspoon salt

½ teaspoon pepper

2 tablespoons olive oil

¼ cup finely chopped shallots

1 teaspoon finely chopped garlic cloves

½ cup beef broth (from 32-oz carton)

½ cup dry white wine

⅔ cup whipping cream

¼ cup plus 2 tablespoons crumbled blue cheese (1½ oz)

2 tablespoons finely chopped chives

1 Sprinkle beef steaks with salt and pepper. In 8-inch skillet, heat 1 tablespoon olive oil over medium-high heat. Cook steaks 6 to 8 minutes, turning once, until browned on both sides and desired doneness (160°F for medium doneness).

2 In another 8-inch skillet, heat remaining 1 tablespoon olive oil over medium heat. Add shallots; cook about 3 minutes, stirring occasionally, until tender. Add garlic; stir 1 minute. Add broth and wine; heat to boiling. Cook 5 minutes. Add whipping cream; heat to boiling. Reduce heat. Simmer 7 to 10 minutes or until slightly thickened. Beat in ¼ cup of the blue cheese with whisk until smooth.

3 Pour sauce over steaks; garnish with remaining 2 tablespoons crumbled blue cheese and the chives.

1 Serving: Calories 730; Total Fat 56g (Saturated Fat 26g, Trans Fat 1.5g); Cholesterol 215mg; Sodium 1170mg; Total Carbohydrate 8g (Dietary Fiber 1g); Protein 44g **Exchanges:** ½ Other Carbohydrate, 6 Lean Meat, ½ High-Fat Meat, 7 Fat **Carbohydrate Choices:** ½

Swap It Blue cheese comes in a large variety of flavors. While Danish blue is mild and creamy, Roquefort can be much stronger in flavor, so choose the cheese that suits your taste best.

Swap It Sliced green onions can be substituted for the chives in this recipe.

Black *and* Bleu Steak Skillet

Prep Time: 25 Minutes • Start to Finish: 25 Minutes • 2 servings

3   tablespoons olive oil

1   boneless beef strip steak
     (about 12 oz), trimmed

1   teaspoon Montreal steak
     grill seasoning

1   medium shallot,
     thinly sliced

3   tablespoons
     balsamic vinegar

1   tablespoon red
     wine vinegar

1   teaspoon honey

4   cups baby arugula

½   cup crumbled blue cheese
     (2 oz)

1 In 10-inch skillet, heat 1 tablespoon of the oil over medium heat. Sprinkle beef steak with grill seasoning. Add to skillet; cook 9 to 11 minutes, turning once, until browned on both sides and desired doneness (160°F for medium doneness). Place on cutting board, let stand 5 minutes. Cut steak into ¼-inch slices.

2 Meanwhile, add shallot to same skillet; cook over medium heat 1 minute, stirring constantly. Reduce heat to low; add balsamic vinegar, red wine vinegar, remaining 2 tablespoons olive oil and the honey; stir constantly 1 to 2 minutes or until shallots are coated and vinegar mixture is blended. Remove from heat.

3 Place arugula on serving plate; top with steak slices, shallots and blue cheese.

1 Serving: Calories 620; Total Fat 42g (Saturated Fat 14g, Trans Fat 1g); Cholesterol 145mg; Sodium 580mg; Total Carbohydrate 10g (Dietary Fiber 0g); Protein 49g **Exchanges:** 1½ Vegetable, 6½ Medium-Fat Meat, 2 Fat **Carbohydrate Choices:** ½

Kitchen Tip Pair this steak skillet with a side of potatoes and red wine for a cozy dinner for two.

Swap It Montreal steak grill seasoning is readily available in the spice aisle of your grocery store. If you just want to use salt and pepper, substitute ¼ teaspoon salt and ¼ teaspoon ground pepper for the seasoning blend.

Grilled Southwestern Pork Chops

Prep Time: 15 Minutes • Start to Finish: 20 Minutes • 4 servings

SOUTHWESTERN RUB

- 1 tablespoon chili powder
- 1 teaspoon ground cumin
- ¼ teaspoon salt
- ¼ teaspoon ground red pepper (cayenne)
- 1 clove garlic, finely chopped
- 1 tablespoon vegetable oil

PORK

- 4 boneless pork loin or rib chops, about 1 inch thick (about 2 lb), trimmed of excess fat

1 Heat gas or charcoal grill. In small bowl, mix rub ingredients. Rub mixture evenly on both sides of pork chops.

2 Place pork chops on grill over medium heat. Cover grill; cook 8 to 10 minutes, turning once, until pork is no longer pink and meat thermometer inserted in center reads 145°F. Let stand at least 3 minutes before serving.

1 Serving: Calories 340; Total Fat 14g (Saturated Fat 4g, Trans Fat 0g); Cholesterol 140mg; Sodium 330mg; Total Carbohydrate 2g (Dietary Fiber 0g); Protein 53g **Exchanges:** 7½ Very Lean Meat, 2 Fat **Carbohydrate Choices:** 0

Kitchen Tip Rubs are simple ways to season meats—just sprinkle on the seasoning mixture and rub it into the meat with your fingers. Because this rub has oil in it, it's known as a wet rub rather than a dry rub.

Pork Chops *and* Apples

Prep Time: 10 Minutes • Start to Finish: 1 Hour 5 Minutes • 2 servings

1   medium unpeeled cooking apple, sliced

2   tablespoons packed brown sugar

¼   teaspoon ground cinnamon

2   bone-in pork rib chops, ½ to ¾ inch thick (about ½ lb)

1 Heat oven to 350°F. Place apples in ungreased 1½-quart casserole. Sprinkle with brown sugar and cinnamon.

2 Spray 8- or 10-inch skillet with cooking spray; heat over medium heat 1 to 2 minutes. Add pork chops; cook about 5 minutes, turning once, until light brown. Place pork in single layer on apples.

3 Cover; bake about 45 minutes or until pork is no longer pink in center and apples are tender.

1 Serving: Calories 350; Total Fat 8g (Saturated Fat 2.5g, Trans Fat 0g); Cholesterol 110mg; Sodium 100mg; Total Carbohydrate 26g (Dietary Fiber 2g); Protein 41g **Exchanges:** ½ Fruit, 1 Other Carbohydrate, 6 Very Lean Meat, 1 Fat **Carbohydrate Choices:** 2

Kitchen Tip Some common cooking apples are Cortland, Northern Spy, Rome Beauty, Winesap, Golden Delicious and Granny Smith.

Baked Monte Cristo Sandwiches

Prep Time: 10 Minutes • Start to Finish: 35 Minutes • 3 servings

1 cup Original Bisquick mix

⅓ cup milk

1 egg white

2 oz Swiss cheese, thinly sliced

3 oz deli ham, very thinly sliced

3 oz deli turkey, very thinly sliced

3 tablespoons seedless strawberry jam or preserves

Powdered sugar

1 Heat oven to 400°F. Line 8 × 4-inch loaf pan with foil, leaving foil overhanging at 2 opposite sides of pan; spray foil with cooking spray. In small bowl, stir Bisquick mix, milk and egg white until blended.

2 Spread half of dough in bottom of pan. Top with half each of the cheese, ham and turkey. Spread strawberry jam over turkey to within ½ inch of sides of pan. Top with remaining ham, turkey and cheese. Spread remaining dough over cheese to sides of pan.

3 Bake, uncovered, about 25 minutes or until golden brown. Let stand 5 minutes before serving. Sprinkle generously with powdered sugar. Serve warm.

1 Serving: Calories 360; Total Fat 11g (Saturated Fat 4.5g, Trans Fat 0g); Cholesterol 50mg; Sodium 1170mg; Total Carbohydrate 44g (Dietary Fiber 2g); Protein 21g **Exchanges:** 1½ Starch, 1½ Other Carbohydrate, 2 Lean Meat, ½ High-Fat Meat **Carbohydrate Choices:** 3

Kitchen Tip Serve with additional strawberry jam if you like.

Kitchen Tip The foil-lined pan provides easy pan removal and cleanup. If you don't have foil on hand, you can spray your loaf pan with cooking spray.

Ham _and_ Cheese–Stuffed Pork Chops _with_ Dijon Sauce

Prep Time: 30 Minutes • Start to Finish: 45 Minutes • 2 servings

PORK CHOPS

- 2 bone-in pork rib chops, 1½ inches thick
- ½ teaspoon salt
- ½ teaspoon pepper
- 2 thin slices deli Swiss cheese (1 oz each)
- 2 thin slices deli ham (1 oz each)
- ¼ cup all-purpose flour
- 1 egg
- ⅔ cup plain panko crispy bread crumbs
- 3 tablespoons vegetable oil

SAUCE

- 1 tablespoon olive oil
- ¼ cup finely chopped shallots
- ¾ cup chicken broth (from 32-oz carton)
- ½ cup dry white wine
- ½ cup whipping cream
- 2 tablespoons Dijon mustard
- 1 tablespoon chopped fresh parsley leaves

1 Heat oven to 400°F. Grease 15 × 10 × 1-inch pan. Using small sharp knife, make pocket in each pork chop by cutting into side of chop toward bone. Sprinkle chops with ¼ teaspoon salt and ¼ teaspoon pepper.

2 Place Swiss cheese slices on top of ham slices, and starting from one of the short ends, roll up. Tuck 1 ham and cheese roll into each pork chop pocket.

3 In shallow bowl, stir flour, remaining ¼ teaspoon salt and ¼ teaspoon pepper. Coat both sides of pork chops with flour mixture. In another shallow bowl, beat egg with whisk to blend. In another shallow bowl, place bread crumbs. Dip pork chops into beaten egg; turn to coat. Dip in bread crumb mixture, coating completely.

4 In 12-inch skillet, heat vegetable oil over medium-high heat. Add pork chops; cook 4 to 5 minutes or until golden brown, turning once. Transfer to prepared pan. Bake 18 to 20 minutes or until pork is no long pink in center and meat thermometer inserted in center reads 145°F.

5 Meanwhile, in 8-inch skillet, heat olive oil over medium-high heat. Add shallots; cook 2 to 3 minutes, stirring occasionally, until tender. Add broth and wine; cook 10 to 15 minutes or until reduced by three-fourths. Stir in cream; cook 3 to 4 minutes, stirring occasionally, until slightly thickened. Stir in mustard and parsley. Remove from heat.

6 Place pork chops on serving plates. Serve with sauce.

1 Serving: Calories 920; Total Fat 60g (Saturated Fat 23g, Trans Fat 1g); Cholesterol 255mg; Sodium 1810mg; Total Carbohydrate 48g (Dietary Fiber 2g); Protein 44g **Exchanges:** 2 Starch, 1 Other Carbohydrate, 4½ Lean Meat, 1 High-Fat Meat, 7½ Fat **Carbohydrate Choices:** 3

Swap It Gruyère cheese can be substituted for the Swiss cheese in this recipe.

Kitchen Tip When choosing ham for this dish, look for a variety that is not overly sweet. Black Forest ham is a good choice because it has a nice smoky flavor without a sweet glaze.

122 RIGHT-SIZE RECIPES

Creamy Smothered Ranch Pork Chops

Prep Time: 30 Minutes • Start to Finish: 30 Minutes • 2 servings

1 tablespoon butter

1 small onion, halved and cut into ¼-inch slices (1 cup)

2 bone-in pork loin chops, ¾ inch thick (about 1 lb), trimmed of fat

⅛ teaspoon pepper

1 cup chicken broth (from 32-oz carton)

⅓ cup chive and onion cream cheese spread (from 8-oz container)

2 teaspoons ranch dressing and seasoning mix (from 1-oz package)

2 cups cooked egg noodles

Chopped fresh chives, if desired

1 In 10-inch nonstick skillet, heat butter over medium-high heat. Add onion; cook 5 to 7 minutes, stirring frequently, until browned and tender. Spoon mixture onto plate.

2 Sprinkle pork chops with pepper. Add to same skillet; cook over medium-high heat 5 to 7 minutes, turning once, until browned and no longer pink in center. Remove from skillet to plate with onion; cover and keep warm.

3 Add chicken broth, cream cheese spread and ranch seasoning to skillet. Cook 3 to 4 minutes, stirring frequently, until bubbly and slightly thickened. Add pork chops and onion back to skillet; cook 2 to 3 minutes or until heated through.

4 Cool 5 minutes before serving to allow sauce to thicken. Serve with egg noodles. Garnish with chopped chives.

1 Serving: Calories 680; Total Fat 32g (Saturated Fat 15g, Trans Fat 0.5g); Cholesterol 205mg; Sodium 1390mg; Total Carbohydrate 50g (Dietary Fiber 2g); Protein 47g **Exchanges:** 2 Starch, 1 Other Carbohydrate, ½ Vegetable, 5½ Lean Meat, 3 Fat **Carbohydrate Choices:** 3

Use It Up Chive and onion cream cheese spread is found in the refrigerated aisle near the regular cream cheese. Leftover spread is delicious as a dip or on baked potatoes.

Fall Pork Dinner

Prep Time: 20 Minutes • Start to Finish: 1 Hour 5 Minutes • 3 servings

¼ cup packed brown sugar

½ teaspoon ground cinnamon

1 tablespoon cold butter, cut up

½ small acorn squash

1 small unpeeled red cooking apple

⅓ cup all-purpose flour

½ teaspoon seasoned salt

⅛ teaspoon pepper

5 saltine crackers, crushed

1 egg white or 2 tablespoons fat-free egg product

1 tablespoon water

3 boneless pork loin chops, ½ inch thick (about ¾ lb)

1 Heat oven to 350°F. In small bowl, mix brown sugar, cinnamon and butter until crumbly; set aside. Cut squash into ½-inch rings. Cut rings in half; remove seeds. Cut apple into chunks.

2 In shallow dish, stir flour, seasoned salt, pepper and cracker crumbs. In another shallow dish, mix egg white and water. Dip pork into egg mixture, then coat with flour mixture.

3 Spray 10-inch skillet with cooking spray; heat over medium-high heat. Cook pork in skillet 6 to 8 minutes, turning once, until coating is brown. Place pork in ungreased 8-inch square (2-quart) glass baking dish. Arrange squash and apples around pork. Sprinkle with brown sugar mixture.

4 Bake, uncovered, 40 to 45 minutes or until squash is tender and pork is no longer pink in center.

1 Serving: Calories 440; Total Fat 18g (Saturated Fat 7g, Trans Fat 0g); Cholesterol 80mg; Sodium 370mg; Total Carbohydrate 44g (Dietary Fiber 3g); Protein 27g **Exchanges:** 2 Starch, 1 Other Carbohydrate, 3 Lean Meat, 1½ Fat **Carbohydrate Choices:** 3

Swap It If you don't have seasoned salt, use ½ teaspoon regular salt and a dash of paprika instead.

Barbecued Pork Chops

Prep Time: 10 Minutes • Start to Finish: 6 Hours 10 Minutes • 2 servings

2 boneless pork loin chops,
1 inch thick (about ¾ lb),
trimmed of fat

2 slices onion

1 clove garlic,
finely chopped

½ cup barbecue sauce

1 teaspoon cornstarch

1 tablespoon cold water

1 Spray 2- to 3½-quart slow cooker with cooking spray. Place pork chops in slow cooker. Top each with onion slice; sprinkle with garlic. Pour barbecue sauce over pork.

2 Cover; cook on Low heat setting 5 to 6 hours.

3 Remove pork from slow cooker to serving platter. Top each with onion slice; cover to keep warm.

4 In 2-cup microwavable measuring cup, blend cornstarch and water until smooth. Stir in liquid from slow cooker. Microwave uncovered on High 1 to 2 minutes, stirring once halfway through cooking, until mixture boils and thickens slightly. Serve with pork chops.

1 Serving: Calories 370; Total Fat 9g (Saturated Fat 2.5g, Trans Fat 0g); Cholesterol 110mg; Sodium 810mg; Total Carbohydrate 31g (Dietary Fiber 0g); Protein 42g **Exchanges:** 2 Other Carbohydrate, 6 Very Lean Meat, 1 Fat **Carbohydrate Choices:** 2

Kitchen Tip Green beans and roasted red potatoes would pair nicely with these barbecued pork chops.

Pork Tenderloin *with* Rosemary

Prep Time: 5 Minutes • Start to Finish: 35 Minutes • 3 servings

1 **pork tenderloin (about ¾ lb)**

¼ **teaspoon salt**

⅛ **teaspoon pepper**

1½ **teaspoons finely chopped fresh rosemary leaves or ½ teaspoon dried rosemary leaves, crushed**

1 **clove garlic, finely chopped**

1 Heat oven to 425°F. Spray 8-inch square pan with cooking spray.

2 Sprinkle pork on all sides with salt and pepper. Rub with rosemary and garlic. Place pork in pan. Insert ovenproof meat thermometer so tip is in thickest part of pork.

3 Bake, uncovered, 20 to 30 minutes or until thermometer reads 145°F. Cover loosely with foil; let stand 3 minutes. Cut pork crosswise into thin slices.

1 Serving: Calories 150; Total Fat 5g (Saturated Fat 1.5g, Trans Fat 0g); Cholesterol 70mg; Sodium 250mg; Total Carbohydrate 0g (Dietary Fiber 0g); Protein 26g **Exchanges:** 3½ Very Lean Meat, ½ Fat **Carbohydrate Choices:** 0

Kitchen Tip When using dried rosemary, crumble the leaves in the palm of your hand to release more flavor before rubbing them over the pork.

Rolled Pork Tenderloin and Sweet Potatoes

Prep Time: 20 Minutes • Start to Finish: 5 Hours 20 Minutes • 2 servings

2 tablespoons packed brown sugar

½ teaspoon Caribbean jerk seasoning

1 pork tenderloin (¾ lb)

1 small apple, thinly sliced

2 tablespoons sweetened dried cranberries

1 large dark-orange sweet potato (about 1 lb), peeled, cut into ½-inch-thick slices

2 tablespoons water

2 teaspoons all-purpose flour

1 Spray 2½- to 3½-quart slow cooker with cooking spray. In small bowl, stir together brown sugar and Caribbean jerk seasoning.

2 Between pieces of plastic wrap or waxed paper, place pork tenderloin; gently pound with flat side of meat mallet or rolling pin until about ½ inch thick. Sprinkle with 1 teaspoon of the brown sugar mixture. Top evenly with apple slices and cranberries. Starting with one short side, roll up; secure with string.

3 Place sweet potato slices in slow cooker. Top with pork roll. Sprinkle with remaining brown sugar mixture. Cover and cook on Low heat setting 4 to 5 hours.

4 About 5 minutes before serving, in 1-cup microwavable measuring cup, stir together water and flour. Remove pork to cutting board. Remove sweet potatoes to serving platter. Stir juices from slow cooker into flour mixture. Microwave on High 30 to 60 seconds, stirring once, until mixture boils and thickens slightly. Cut pork into slices; place over sweet potatoes. Pour sauce over top.

1 Serving: Calories 450; Total Fat 8g (Saturated Fat 2.5g, Trans Fat 0g); Cholesterol 105mg; Sodium 190mg; Total Carbohydrate 53g (Dietary Fiber 5g); Protein 40g **Exchanges:** 1½ Starch, ½ Fruit, 1½ Other Carbohydrate, 5 Very Lean Meat, 1 Fat **Carbohydrate Choices:** 3½

Swap It The dried cranberries are delicious in this recipe, but dried cherries or cut-up apricots would be yummy too.

Honey Barbecue Pork Roast *with* Carrots

Prep Time: 5 Minutes • Start to Finish: 5 Hours 35 Minutes • 2 servings

½ lb boneless pork loin or sirloin roast, trimmed of fat

2 tablespoons barbecue sauce

2 teaspoons honey

1½ teaspoons balsamic vinegar

½ teaspoon soy sauce

⅛ teaspoon ginger

Dash pepper

⅔ cup frozen honey glazed carrots, thawed (from a 10-oz package)

1 Spray 1½-quart slow cooker with cooking spray. In cooker, place pork roast. In 1-cup measuring cup, stir together barbecue sauce, honey, balsamic vinegar, soy sauce, ginger and pepper; pour over pork.

2 Cover; cook on Low heat setting 4 to 5 hours.

3 Place carrots around pork. Increase heat setting to High. Cover; cook about 30 minutes or until carrots are crisp-tender. Using a slotted spoon, remove pork from cooker to cutting board. Cut pork into slices; place on serving platter. Top pork with sauce and carrots.

1 Serving: Calories 260; Total Fat 10g (Saturated Fat 3.5g, Trans Fat 0g); Cholesterol 70mg; Sodium 350mg; Total Carbohydrate 19g (Dietary Fiber 1g); Protein 25g **Exchanges:** 1 Other Carbohydrate, 3½ Lean Meat **Carbohydrate Choices:** 1

Kitchen Tip If desired, thinly slice 1 small onion and place in slow cooker. Place pork on top of onion and cook as directed.

Swap It If desired, substitute ¾ lb thick-cut pork chops for pork loin roast.

Spicy Pork Carnitas Soup

Prep Time: 20 Minutes • Start to Finish: 35 Minutes • 3 servings (1⅓ cups each)

1   tablespoon olive oil

1   medium onion, halved, thinly sliced

1   green bell pepper, cut into strips

1   cup chicken broth (from 32-oz carton)

½   cup beer

1   teaspoon chili powder

¼   teaspoon salt

¼   teaspoon ground cumin

1   can (10.5 oz) diced tomatoes with green chiles, undrained

2   boneless pork loin chops, trimmed of fat and cut into ½-inch cubes (about 8 oz)

1   tablespoon chopped fresh cilantro

1   tablespoon fresh lime juice

   Cilantro leaves, if desired

1 In 2-quart saucepan, heat olive oil over medium heat. Add onion and pepper; cook 4 to 5 minutes or until vegetables are tender. Stir in chicken broth, beer, chili powder, salt, cumin and tomatoes.

2 Heat to boiling; reduce heat. Cover and simmer 5 minutes. Stir in pork; cover and simmer 5 to 8 minutes or until pork is no longer pink in center. Stir in chopped cilantro and lime juice. Garnish with cilantro leaves.

1 Serving: Calories 260; Total Fat 10g (Saturated Fat 2.5g, Trans Fat 0g); Cholesterol 75mg; Sodium 810mg; Total Carbohydrate 11g (Dietary Fiber 2g); Protein 29g **Exchanges:** 2 Vegetable, 3½ Lean Meat **Carbohydrate Choices:** 1

Swap It You can substitute boneless skinless chicken breasts or thighs for the pork. Use ½ pound of whichever you prefer. Also, you can use red, yellow or orange bell peppers instead of the green bell peppers.

Kitchen Tip For a bit of crunch, garnish this soup with fried tortilla strips. Look for them in the produce or deli section of your grocery store.

Sausage *and* Wild Mushroom Skillet Pizza

Prep Time: 45 Minutes • Start to Finish: 1 Hour 45 Minutes • 2 servings

CRUST

- 1 package regular active dry yeast
- 1 cup warm water (105°F to 115°F)
- 2½ cups all-purpose flour
- 2 tablespoons olive oil
- 2 tablespoons butter, softened
- 1½ teaspoons salt
- 1 teaspoon sugar

TOPPINGS

- 1 tablespoon plus 1 teaspoon olive oil
- 4 oz sliced cremini mushrooms (about 1 cup)
- 4 oz bulk mild Italian sausage
- ⅓ cup whipping cream
- ½ teaspoon chopped fresh thyme leaves
- ⅓ cup crushed tomatoes (from 14.5-oz can)
- 1 clove garlic, finely chopped
- ¼ teaspoon crushed red pepper flakes
- 1 cup shredded mozzarella cheese (4 oz)

1 In medium bowl, dissolve yeast in warm water. With wooden spoon, stir in flour, 2 tablespoons oil, the butter, salt and sugar.

2 Sprinkle flour lightly on work surface. Place dough on floured surface. Knead 5 to 10 minutes, sprinkling surface with more flour only if dough starts to stick, until dough is smooth and springy but still soft. Spray large bowl with cooking spray. Place dough in bowl, turning dough to grease all sides. Cover bowl loosely with plastic wrap; let rise in warm place about 1 hour or until doubled in size.

3 Heat oven to 450°F. In 9-inch cast-iron skillet, heat 1 tablespoon of the oil over medium-high heat. Add mushrooms; cook 3 to 4 minutes, stirring occasionally, until browned. Spoon mushrooms into small bowl. Add sausage to skillet; cook 3 to 5 minutes, breaking sausage up with back of spoon, until no longer pink. Add whipping cream and thyme; cook 1 to 2 minutes or until liquid is almost evaporated. Spoon into bowl with mushrooms. Allow skillet to cool; wipe out with paper towel.

4 Brush same skillet with 1 teaspoon oil. In small bowl, mix tomatoes, garlic and pepper flakes.

5 Gently push fist into dough to deflate. Place half of dough in skillet. Gently push up side of skillet, creating an even crust on bottom and side. Spread tomato mixture over bottom of crust. Top with mushroom mixture and mozzarella cheese. Freeze other half of dough to use another time.

6 Bake 15 to 20 minutes or until crust is golden brown and cheese is melted and lightly browned.

1 Serving: Calories 950; Total Fat 57g (Saturated Fat 24g, Trans Fat 1g); Cholesterol 120mg; Sodium 1910mg; Total Carbohydrate 74g (Dietary Fiber 4g); Protein 33g **Exchanges:** 1½ Starch, 3 Other Carbohydrate, 2 Vegetable, 2 Medium-Fat Meat, 1½ High-Fat Meat, 7 Fat **Carbohydrate Choices:** 5

To freeze remaining pizza dough for up to 3 months, wrap in plastic wrap, and place in resealable freezer bag. When ready to use, put dough in refrigerator to thaw at least 12 hours. Just before making pizza, let dough stand on countertop 30 minutes.

Italian Sausage Lasagna

Prep Time: 25 Minutes • Start to Finish: 1 Hour 15 Minutes • 4 servings

1 cup shredded mozzarella cheese (4 oz)

1 cup whole-milk ricotta cheese (from 15-oz container)

2 tablespoons butter

½ lb bulk mild Italian sausage

½ cup diced red onion

½ teaspoon crushed red pepper flakes

1½ cups tomato basil pasta sauce (from 26-oz jar)

4 no-boil lasagna noodles (from 8-oz package)

¼ cup shredded Parmesan cheese

2 tablespoons thinly sliced fresh basil leaves, if desired

1 Heat oven to 425°F. Spray 8 × 4-inch loaf pan with cooking spray. In medium bowl, mix mozzarella and ricotta cheeses; set aside.

2 In 10-inch nonstick skillet, melt butter over medium-high heat. Cook sausage, onion and pepper flakes in butter 5 to 7 minutes, stirring frequently, until sausage is cooked through and onion is tender; drain. Return to skillet; stir in sauce.

3 Spread rounded ½ cup sauce mixture in bottom of loaf pan. Top with 1 lasagna noodle. Top with rounded ½ cup ricotta mixture. Pour rounded ½ cup sauce mixture over ricotta mixture. Top with 1 lasagna noodle. Top with rounded ½ cup ricotta mixture, followed by rounded ½ cup sauce mixture. Top with 1 lasagna noodle, followed by remaining ricotta mixture. Top with 1 lasagna noodle, then with remaining sauce mixture. Top with Parmesan cheese.

4 Cover with foil; bake 20 minutes. Remove cover; bake 15 to 20 minutes longer or until pasta is tender and mixture is bubbling at edges. Let stand 10 minutes. Top with basil.

1 Serving: Calories 550; Total Fat 33g (Saturated Fat 17g, Trans Fat 1g); Cholesterol 95mg; Sodium 1080mg; Total Carbohydrate 32g (Dietary Fiber 3g); Protein 29g **Exchanges:** 2 Starch, ½ Vegetable, 2 Medium-Fat Meat, 1 High-Fat Meat, 3 Fat **Carbohydrate Choices:** 2

Swap It Two 4-ounce Italian sausage links work well as a substitute for the bulk sausage. Just remove the casings before cooking.

Kitchen Tip This delicious recipe makes just enough that you can have an additional serving or two without dealing with an entire large pan of lasagna. Heat it up at work for a delicious homemade lunch or enjoy it for dinner later in the week when your night is a busy one.

MEATLESS

Cheesy Cauliflower Crusted Rosemary *and* Tomato Pizza

Prep Time: 20 Minutes • Start to Finish: 55 Minutes • 2 servings

CRUST

- 1 bag (12 oz) frozen riced cauliflower
- 1 egg
- ⅓ cup shredded mozzarella cheese
- 2 tablespoons grated Parmesan cheese
- ½ teaspoon salt
- Cooking spray

TOPPINGS

- ¼ cup pizza sauce (from 14-oz jar)
- ¾ cup shredded mozzarella cheese
- 2 teaspoons chopped fresh rosemary leaves
- 1 Roma tomato, thinly sliced
- 1 thin slice red onion, separated into rings
- 1 tablespoon grated Parmesan cheese

1 Move oven rack to the lowest position. Heat oven to 450°F. Line cookie sheet with cooking parchment paper; spray with cooking spray. Microwave cauliflower as directed on package. Drain in colander. Cool 10 minutes. Using paper towels, press out as much moisture as possible.

2 In medium bowl, combine cauliflower, egg, ⅓ cup mozzarella cheese, 2 tablespoons Parmesan cheese and salt; mix well. Using hands, press cauliflower mixture into 10-inch circle on cookie sheet; spray with cooking spray.

3 Bake 18 to 20 minutes or until golden brown. Spread crust with pizza sauce. Top with ½ cup of the mozzarella cheese. Sprinkle with fresh rosemary. Top with tomatoes and red onion rings. Sprinkle with remaining ¼ cup mozzarella cheese and 1 tablespoon Parmesan cheese.

4 Return to oven; bake 5 minutes longer or until cheese is melted. Let stand 5 minutes. To serve, cut into wedges.

1 Serving: Calories 320; Total Fat 18g (Saturated Fat 10g, Trans Fat 0.5g); Cholesterol 140mg; Sodium 1330mg; Total Carbohydrate 15g (Dietary Fiber 4g); Protein 25g **Exchanges:** 2½ Vegetable, 3 Medium-Fat Meat, ½ Fat **Carbohydrate Choices:** 1

Use It Up If you have some leftover Alfredo pasta sauce, you can substitute it for the pizza sauce.

Swap It This cauliflower crust makes a great base for other toppings like fresh basil leaves, bell pepper strips, sliced mushrooms, thin slices of fresh mozzarella cheese, garbanzo beans or chopped artichoke hearts.

Quick Dinner Nachos

Prep Time: 15 Minutes • Start to Finish: 15 Minutes • 3 servings

1 can (15.5 oz) pinto beans, rinsed, drained

2 cups cubed Mexican pasteurized prepared cheese product with jalapeño peppers (8 oz)

2 to 3 tablespoons milk

6 cups tortilla chips

¼ cup sliced ripe olives

¾ cup chopped seeded tomato

⅓ cup sour cream

¼ cup chopped fresh cilantro

1 In medium saucepan, combine beans and cheese; cook over medium heat until cheese is melted, stirring frequently. Stir in milk, 1 tablespoon at a time, until desired consistency.

2 Place 2 cups chips on each individual serving plate. Spoon about ⅔ cup bean mixture over chips. Top each with olives, tomato, sour cream and cilantro. Serve immediately.

1 Serving: Calories 790; Total Fat 40g (Saturated Fat 17g, Trans Fat 1g); Cholesterol 100mg; Sodium 1870mg; Total Carbohydrate 77g (Dietary Fiber 10g); Protein 29g **Exchanges:** 4 Starch, 1 Other Carbohydrate, 1 Vegetable, 2 High-Fat Meat, 4½ Fat **Carbohydrate Choices:** 5

Swap It Black beans can be used in place of pinto beans.

Kitchen Tip For heartier nachos, add 1 cup crumbled cooked ground beef or shredded cooked chicken.

Nacho Party Pizza

Prep Time: 10 Minutes • Start to Finish: 30 Minutes • 2 servings

1   **frozen crisp crust pepperoni or cheese pizza (9.8 oz)**

⅓   **cup black beans (from 15-oz can), rinsed, drained**

⅓   **cup shredded Cheddar cheese (1.5 oz)**

⅓   **cup chopped tomato**

⅓   **cup coarsely crushed nacho-flavored tortilla chips**

2   **tablespoons ranch dressing**

½   **teaspoon red pepper sauce**

1 Heat oven to 450°F. Line cookie sheet with foil. Spray with cooking spray.

2 Place frozen pizza on cookie sheet. Top with beans and cheese.

3 Bake 15 to 17 minutes or until center is thoroughly heated and cheese is melted. Remove pizza from oven. Sprinkle with tomato and tortilla chips.

4 In small bowl, mix dressing and pepper sauce. Drizzle over pizza. Serve with additional tortilla chips, if desired.

1 Serving: Calories 610; Total Fat 35g (Saturated Fat 10g, Trans Fat 0g); Cholesterol 35mg; Sodium 1180mg; Total Carbohydrate 54g (Dietary Fiber 6g); Protein 19g **Exchanges:** 2½ Starch, 1 Other Carbohydrate, ½ Vegetable, 1½ High-Fat Meat, 4½ Fat **Carbohydrate Choices:** 3½

Swap It Feel free to vary the ingredients on the pizza to meet your nacho preferences.

Slow-Cooker Couscous-Stuffed Peppers

Prep Time: 15 Minutes • Start to Finish: 6 Hours 15 Minutes • 4 servings

4 large bell peppers

½ lb extra-lean (at least 90%) ground beef

1 medium onion, chopped (½ cup)

1 clove garlic, finely chopped

2 cans (8 oz each) tomato sauce

½ teaspoon salt

½ teaspoon ground cumin

¼ teaspoon ground cinnamon

⅛ teaspoon ground red pepper (cayenne)

⅔ cup uncooked couscous

1 cup water

Pine nuts, if desired

1 Cut thin slice from stem end of each bell pepper to remove top of pepper. Remove seeds and membranes; rinse peppers.

2 In 10-inch skillet, cook beef, onion and garlic over medium-high heat 5 to 7 minutes, stirring occasionally, until beef is thoroughly cooked; drain. Stir in tomato sauce, salt, cumin, cinnamon and red pepper. Stir in couscous. Divide beef mixture evenly among bell peppers.

3 Pour water into oval 3½-quart slow cooker. Stand filled bell peppers upright in cooker.

4 Cover; cook on Low heat setting 4 to 6 hours or until peppers are tender. Garnish with pine nuts.

1 Serving: Calories 280; Total Fat 5g (Saturated Fat 2g, Trans Fat 0g); Cholesterol 35mg; Sodium 870mg; Total Carbohydrate 39g (Dietary Fiber 6g); Protein 17g **Exchanges:** 1½ Starch, ½ Fruit, 1½ Vegetable, 1½ Very Lean Meat, ½ Fat **Carbohydrate Choices:** 2½

Swap It If you like couscous, try whole wheat couscous, now available at most grocery stores.

Kitchen Tip To reheat the remaining 2 peppers and filling, place on microwavable plate and cover loosely with plastic wrap. Microwave on 70% power 1½ to 2 minutes or until hot.

Spinach–White Bean Enchiladas

Prep Time: 20 Minutes • Start to Finish: 50 Minutes • 2 servings (2 enchiladas each)

1 can (10 oz) green chile enchilada sauce

2 teaspoons vegetable oil

2 medium green onions, thinly sliced (2 tablespoons)

½ teaspoon finely chopped garlic

¾ cup chopped fresh spinach leaves

¾ cup great northern beans (from 15-oz can), rinsed, drained

1 can (4 oz) diced green chiles

½ cup shredded Monterey Jack cheese

4 flour tortillas (7 or 8 inch)

¼ cup diced tomatoes

2 tablespoons chopped fresh cilantro

   Sour cream, if desired

1 Heat oven to 375°F. Spray bottom and sides of 8-inch square (2-quart) glass baking dish with cooking spray. Spread ¼ cup of the enchilada sauce in bottom of baking dish.

2 In 8-inch nonstick skillet, heat oil over medium heat. Add green onions and garlic; cook 2 to 3 minutes or until onions are tender. Add spinach; stir just until spinach starts to wilt; remove from heat. Spoon mixture into medium bowl.

3 Add beans, green chiles, ¼ cup of the cheese and ½ cup enchilada sauce to spinach mixture; mix well. Spoon generous ⅓ cup spinach mixture down center of each tortilla. Roll up tortillas; arrange, seam sides down, in baking dish. Pour remaining enchilada sauce over enchiladas; sprinkle with remaining ¼ cup cheese.

4 Bake, uncovered, 27 to 32 minutes or until bubbling around edges and enchiladas are heated through. Top with diced tomatoes and cilantro. Serve with sour cream.

1 Serving: Calories 630; Total Fat 25g (Saturated Fat 10g, Trans Fat 0g); Cholesterol 25mg; Sodium 2200mg; Total Carbohydrate 80g (Dietary Fiber 9g); Protein 23g **Exchanges:** 4½ Starch, ½ Other Carbohydrate, 1 Vegetable, 1 High-Fat Meat, 3 Fat **Carbohydrate Choices:** 5

Swap It For extra spicy flavor, use pepper Jack cheese in place of Monterey Jack.

Use It Up Give your salad a protein boost by topping with the remaining beans.

Use It Up Make baked tortilla chips with extra tortillas. Heat oven to 350°F. Spray both sides of tortillas with nonstick cooking spray or brush lightly with oil. Sprinkle with salt, if desired. Cut into wedges. Place in single layer on baking pan. Bake 10 minutes or until crisp and just beginning to brown.

Vegetarian Tostadas

Prep Time: 15 Minutes • Start to Finish: 30 Minutes • 2 servings

2 teaspoons vegetable oil

⅔ cup diced
butternut squash

¼ cup diced red onion

¼ cup black beans seasoned
with cumin and chili spices
(from 15-oz can), drained

2 frozen buttermilk or
southern-style biscuits
(from 25-oz bag)

¼ cup shredded Mexican
cheese blend (1 oz)

1 Heat oven to 375°F. Spray cookie sheet with cooking spray. In 8-inch skillet, heat oil over medium-high heat. Add squash and onion; cook 4 to 5 minutes or until squash is tender. Remove from heat; stir in black beans. Set aside.

2 Place frozen biscuits on microwavable plate. Microwave uncovered on High 15 seconds; turn over. Microwave about 10 seconds longer or until biscuits are softened.

3 Place biscuits on cookie sheet. Press each to 5-inch round. Spoon squash mixture evenly over biscuits.

4 Bake 10 minutes; sprinkle with cheese. Bake 5 to 8 minutes longer or until cheese is melted and biscuit edges are lightly browned.

1 Serving: Calories 320; Total Fat 16g (Saturated Fat 5g, Trans Fat 7g); Cholesterol 15mg; Sodium 710mg; Total Carbohydrate 35g (Dietary Fiber 3g); Protein 10g **Exchanges:** 2 Starch, ½ Vegetable, ½ High-Fat Meat, 2 Fat **Carbohydrate Choices:** 2

Swap It You can easily use a milder cheese such as Monterey Jack or Cheddar.

Veggie Burgers *with* Caramelized Onions

Prep Time: 20 Minutes • Start to Finish: 20 Minutes • 2 sandwiches

1 tablespoon olive oil

½ cup thinly sliced sweet onion, such as Walla Walla or Vidalia

4 mushrooms, sliced (about ⅔ cup)

½ teaspoon finely chopped garlic

1 teaspoon balsamic vinegar

1 teaspoon chopped fresh rosemary or ½ teaspoon dried rosemary leaves, crushed

⅛ teaspoon salt

⅛ teaspoon pepper

2 veggie burgers

2 large pretzel buns or hamburger buns, split

4 teaspoons Dijon mustard

½ cup lightly packed baby arugula

2 tomato slices

1 In 8-inch nonstick skillet, heat oil over medium heat. Cook onion, mushrooms and garlic 8 to 10 minutes, stirring frequently, until onion is golden brown. Stir in vinegar, rosemary, salt and pepper. Cook 30 seconds longer or until vinegar coats onion mixture.

2 Meanwhile, heat veggie burgers according to package directions. Spread cut sides of buns with mustard. Place half the arugula on bottom buns. Place burgers over arugula. Divide onion mixture between patties. Top with tomatoes, remaining arugula and tops of buns. Serve immediately.

1 Sandwich: Calories 380; Total Fat 14g (Saturated Fat 2.5g, Trans Fat 0g); Cholesterol 0mg; Sodium 950mg; Total Carbohydrate 45g (Dietary Fiber 6g); Protein 18g **Exchanges:** 2 Starch, ½ Other Carbohydrate, 1½ Vegetable, 1½ Lean Meat, 1½ Fat **Carbohydrate Choices:** 3

Kitchen Tip For an added layer of texture, toast buns before filling. Brush cut sides with about 1 teaspoon butter or olive oil; cook cut side down in the skillet until bottoms are golden brown.

Swap It For meat and cheese lovers, substitute beef burgers and add a slice of Brie cheese during the last few minutes of cooking.

Polenta *and* Spinach–Stuffed Tomatoes

Prep Time: 45 Minutes • Start to Finish: 1 Hour • 2 servings

2 large tomatoes (about ½ lb each)

¼ cup cornmeal

¼ cup water

¼ teaspoon salt

¾ cup boiling water or vegetable broth

½ cup plus 1 teaspoon grated Parmesan cheese

½ cup chopped fresh spinach

1 tablespoon chopped fresh basil leaves

1 Heat oven to 350°F. Cut ¼-inch slice from stem end of each tomato. Use spoon to scoop out pulp; discard. Drain any excess liquid from tomatoes.

2 Place tomatoes in ungreased 8-inch square pan. In 1-quart saucepan, mix cornmeal, ¼ cup water and salt. Stir in ¾ cup boiling water. Cook, stirring constantly with whisk over medium heat until mixture thickens and boils, about 2 minutes. Reduce heat to low.

3 Cover and simmer about 30 minutes, stirring occasionally, until very thick. Stir in ½ cup of the Parmesan cheese, the spinach and basil; cook 1 to 2 minutes or until cheese is melted. Remove from heat. Stir until smooth.

4 Spoon polenta into tomatoes. Bake about 15 minutes or until heated through and tomatoes are slightly soft. Sprinkle each tomato with ½ teaspoon of the remaining Parmesan cheese.

1 Serving: Calories 230; Total Fat 8g (Saturated Fat 5g, Trans Fat 0g); Cholesterol 20mg; Sodium 720mg; Total Carbohydrate 24g (Dietary Fiber 3g); Protein 13g **Exchanges:** 1 Starch, 2 Vegetable, 1 High-Fat Meat **Carbohydrate Choices:** 1½

Swap It If your tomatoes are smaller, use 3 or 4 tomatoes in place of the 2 larger tomatoes. The total weight of the tomatoes should be about 1 pound.

Kitchen Tip If your tomatoes are in season, you will probably be able to remove the core and pulp with a spoon. If the tomatoes are underripe or out of season, you may need to use a paring knife to help you remove the core.

Black Bean–Stuffed Sweet Potatoes

Prep Time: 10 Minutes • Start to Finish: 1 Hour 35 Minutes • 2 servings

2 medium dark-orange sweet potatoes (1⅓ lb)

2 teaspoons vegetable oil

2 tablespoons chipotle mayonnaise

¼ teaspoon salt

¾ cup black beans (from 15-oz can), rinsed, drained

½ cup frozen honey roasted sweet corn and peppers, thawed

2 medium green onions, thinly sliced (2 tablespoons)

4 teaspoons chopped cilantro

¼ cup shredded Monterey Jack cheese

¼ cup crumbled Cotija cheese

1 Heat oven to 375°F. Pierce each sweet potato several times with fork. Rub vegetable oil all over potatoes; wrap loosely in foil. Place on a 12½ × 9½ × 1-inch rimmed baking sheet.

2 Bake 1 hour, or until potatoes are fork-tender. Cool 10 minutes.

3 Cut sweet potatoes in half and spoon potato pulp into medium bowl, leaving ¼-inch pulp next to skins. Add mayonnaise and salt to potato in bowl; mix well. Stir in black beans, corn mixture, 1 tablespoon of the green onions, 3 teaspoons of the cilantro and the shredded cheese.

4 Divide filling mixture into hollowed potato skins; place in same shallow pan.

5 Bake, uncovered, 20 minutes, or until potatoes are heated through. Top with Cotija cheese, remaining 1 tablespoon green onions and remaining 1 teaspoon cilantro.

1 Serving: Calories 500; Total Fat 26g (Saturated Fat 8g, Trans Fat 0g); Cholesterol 35mg; Sodium 1120mg; Total Carbohydrate 50g (Dietary Fiber 12g); Protein 15g **Exchanges:** 2½ Starch, 1 Other Carbohydrate, 1 High-Fat Meat, 3½ Fat **Carbohydrate Choices:** 3

Swap It Substitute another favorite cheese for the Monterey Jack cheese, such as Cheddar or taco cheese; or use Monterey Jack cheese for both the filling and the top if Cotija cheese isn't available.

Use It Up Use the leftover black beans in a soup or salad. Leftover Cotija cheese can be used to top enchiladas, salads or refried beans.

Kitchen Tip Make your own chipotle mayonnaise by combining 2 tablespoons mayonnaise with 1½ to 2 teaspoons finely chopped chipotles in adobo sauce, depending on your preferred level of spiciness.

Cheesy Potato Soup

Prep Time: 25 Minutes • Start to Finish: 7 Hours 45 Minutes • 3 servings

2	slices bacon
¾	cup chopped onion
2½	cups diced peeled russet potatoes (about 3 small)
¼	cup chopped celery
2	cups chicken broth (from 32-oz carton)
¼	teaspoon salt
⅛	teaspoon pepper
¼	cup all-purpose flour
¾	cup half-and-half
1	cup shredded Cheddar cheese (4 oz)

1 In 10-inch skillet, cook bacon over medium heat, turning occasionally, until browned and crisp. Remove bacon from skillet, reserving drippings in skillet. Drain bacon on paper towel. Place in covered container; refrigerate. In same skillet, cook onion in bacon drippings over medium heat 4 to 5 minutes, stirring frequently, until tender.

2 Spray 3- to 3½-quart slow cooker with cooking spray. In cooker, mix onion, potatoes, celery, broth, salt and pepper.

3 Cover; cook on Low heat setting 6 to 7 hours.

4 In small bowl, beat flour and half-and-half with whisk until well blended; stir into soup. Increase heat setting to High. Cover; cook about 20 minutes longer or until thickened. Stir in cheese until well melted. Crumble bacon; sprinkle over soup.

1 Serving: Calories 440; Total Fat 22g (Saturated Fat 13g, Trans Fat 0.5g); Cholesterol 70mg; Sodium 1160mg; Total Carbohydrate 41g (Dietary Fiber 4g); Protein 19g **Exchanges:** 1½ Starch, ½ Other Carbohydrate, 2 Vegetable, 1½ High-Fat Meat, 2 Fat **Carbohydrate Choices:** 3

Swap It One-half cup fat-free half-and-half or milk can be substituted for the half-and-half.

Kitchen Tip Add ¼ cup sliced carrot with the vegetables.

Speedy Ravioli Bake

Prep Time: 20 Minutes • Start to Finish: 30 Minutes • 3 servings (1 cup each)

1   **package (9 oz) refrigerated cheese-filled ravioli**

1½   **cups chunky tomato pasta sauce (from 26-oz jar)**

½   **teaspoon dried basil leaves**

1   **cup shredded mozzarella cheese (4 oz)**

1 Heat oven to 400°F. In 3-quart saucepan, cook ravioli as directed on package; drain and set aside.

2 In same saucepan, mix pasta sauce and basil. Cook over medium heat 3 to 5 minutes, stirring occasionally, until thoroughly heated. Stir in cooked ravioli. Pour into ungreased 8-inch (1½-quart) square glass baking dish. Sprinkle cheese over top.

3 Bake, uncovered, 10 minutes or until sauce is bubbly and cheese is melted.

1 Serving: Calories 380; Total Fat 14g (Saturated Fat 8g, Trans Fat 0g); Cholesterol 105mg; Sodium 1600mg; Total Carbohydrate 40g (Dietary Fiber 6g); Protein 24g **Exchanges:** 1 Starch, 1½ Other Carbohydrate, 3 Very Lean Meat, 2½ Fat **Carbohydrate Choices:** 2½

Swap It This recipe calls for cheese-filled ravioli, but you could substitute any filled ravioli that you like. Why not try spinach-filled or sausage-filled ravioli for a change of flavor?

Creamy Southwestern Corn Chowder

Prep Time: 25 Minutes • Start to Finish: 25 Minutes • 2 servings (1¾ cups each)

2   tablespoons butter

1   medium onion, chopped (½ cup)

¼   cup all-purpose flour

1¾   cups vegetable or chicken broth (from 32-oz carton)

½   teaspoon salt

¼   teaspoon black pepper

⅛   teaspoon ground red pepper (cayenne)

½   cup half-and-half

1   can (11 oz) whole kernel corn with red and green peppers, undrained

2   tablespoons chopped fresh chives

Additional fresh chives, if desired

1 In 2-quart saucepan, melt butter over medium heat. Add onion; cook 3 to 5 minutes, stirring occasionally, until tender.

2 Stir in flour with whisk until well blended. Gradually stir in broth with whisk. Stir in salt, black pepper and red pepper. Heat to boiling. Reduce heat; cook about 5 minutes, stirring frequently, until thickened.

3 Stir in half-and-half, corn and 2 tablespoons chives. Cook until thoroughly heated. Garnish each serving with additional chives.

1 Serving: Calories 420; Total Fat 19g (Saturated Fat 12g, Trans Fat 0.5g); Cholesterol 50mg; Sodium 1740mg; Total Carbohydrate 53g (Dietary Fiber 3g); Protein 8g **Exchanges:** 2½ Starch, 1 Other Carbohydrate, 3½ Fat **Carbohydrate Choices:** 3½

Grilled Cheese–Tomato Soup

Prep Time: 10 Minutes • Start to Finish: 10 Minutes • 2 servings

1   can (19 oz) tomato basil soup

2   packages (1.5 oz each) Colby-Monterey Jack cheese blend cubes (individual size)

½   cup croutons, divided into 2 resealable sandwich-size food storage plastic bags

1 Heat soup as directed on can.

2 For each serving, pour warm soup into small insulated bottle. Pack in lunch bag with cheese cubes, croutons and plastic spoon.

3 At lunchtime, add cheese cubes and croutons to soup.

1 Serving: Calories 350; Total Fat 17g (Saturated Fat 9g, Trans Fat 0g); Cholesterol 40mg; Sodium 1070mg; Total Carbohydrate 37g (Dietary Fiber 2g); Protein 14g **Exchanges:** 2½ Starch, 1 High-Fat Meat, 1½ Fat **Carbohydrate Choices:** 2½

Swap It You can choose to use a different cheese—try Cheddar or mozzarella for variety.

Refrigerator & Freezer Ingredients Storage

Use this handy chart to help keep on top of your kitchen ingredients!

INGREDIENT	REFRIGERATOR (35°F TO 40°F)	FREEZER (0°F OR BELOW)
CONDIMENTS		
Broth (chicken or beef)	3 to 4 days	2 to 3 months
Coconut milk (opened—transfer to glass or plastic container with lid)	1 week	Up to 1 month (blend defrosted coconut milk with immersion blender to restore)
Gravy	3 to 4 days	2 to 3 months
DAIRY PRODUCTS		
Buttermilk, cream and milk	Up to 5 days	Not recommended
Cottage cheese and creamy ricotta	Up to 10 days	Not recommended
Hard cheese	3 to 4 weeks	6 to 8 weeks
Sour cream and yogurt	Up to 1 week	Not recommended
EGGS		
Cooked eggs in shell	1 week	Not recommended
Fresh eggs in shell	2 weeks	Not recommended
LIQUID PASTEURIZED EGGS, EGG SUBSTITUTES		
Opened	3 days	Not recommended
Unopened	10 days	1 year
FATS AND OILS		
Butter	No longer than 2 weeks	No longer than 2 months
LEFTOVERS (COOKED)		
Meat and meat casseroles	3 to 4 days	2 to 3 months
Pizza	3 to 4 days	1 to 2 months
Salads (egg, chicken, ham, tuna and macaroni)	3 to 5 days	Not recommended
Soups and stews	3 to 4 days	2 to 3 months
Stuffing	3 to 4 days	1 month
MEATS (If wrapped in white butcher paper, rewrap tightly in plastic wrap, foil or plastic freezer bags)		
Chops (uncooked) Ground (uncooked)	3 to 5 days 1 to 2 days	4 to 6 months 3 to 4 months
Roasts and steaks (uncooked)	3 to 5 days	6 to 12 months
Cold cuts	3 to 5 days (opened) 2 weeks (unopened)	Not recommended Not recommended
Bacon, cured	5 to 7 days	No longer than 1 month
Hot dogs	1 week (opened) 2 weeks (unopened)	1 to 2 months 1 to 2 months
Ham, whole or half (cooked)	5 to 7 days	1 to 2 months
Ham slices (cooked)	3 to 4 days	1 to 2 months

INGREDIENT	REFRIGERATOR (35°F TO 40°F)	FREEZER (0°F OR BELOW)
Sausage, raw	1 to 2 days	1 to 2 months
Smoked breakfast links, patties	7 days	1 to 2 months
NUTS	6 months	1 year
POULTRY		
Whole including game birds, ducks and geese (uncooked)	1 to 2 days	No longer than 12 months
Cut-up (cooked)	5 to 7 days	No longer than 9 months
Cooked	3 to 4 days	1 to 2 months
SEAFOOD		
Fish (uncooked)	1 to 2 days	3 to 6 months
Fish (breaded, cooked)	Store in freezer	2 to 3 months
Shellfish (uncooked)	1 to 2 days	3 to 4 months
Shellfish (cooked)	3 to 4 days	1 to 2 months

Quick Onion Soup Gratinée

Prep Time: 15 Minutes • Start to Finish: 15 Minutes • 2 servings

1 can (18.5 oz) French onion soup

½ cup shredded Swiss or Gruyère cheese (2 oz)

1 tablespoon grated Parmesan cheese

2 slices (½ inch thick) French bread, toasted

1 In small saucepan, heat soup over medium-high heat until hot, stirring occasionally.

2 Meanwhile, in small bowl, combine cheeses; mix well.

3 Set oven control to broil. To serve, place 2 ovenproof bowls on cookie sheet for easier handling. Ladle soup into bowls. Top each with slice of toasted bread. Sprinkle each with about ¼ cup cheese mixture.

4 Broil 3 to 5 inches from heat for 1 to 3 minutes or until cheese is bubbly.

1 Serving: Calories 270; Total Fat 12g (Saturated Fat 7g, Trans Fat 0g); Cholesterol 35mg; Sodium 1270mg; Total Carbohydrate 26g (Dietary Fiber 1g); Protein 13g **Exchanges:** 1 Starch, ½ Other Carbohydrate, ½ Lean Meat, 1 High-Fat Meat, ½ Fat **Carbohydrate Choices:** 2

Kitchen Tip Gratinée is a French word that refers to food topped with cheese or buttered bread crumbs, then broiled until crispy and brown. Our quick version of the classic French recipe produces a bistro-style supper in minutes.

Kitchen Tip Gruyère is a rich, smooth, firm cheese named for the Gruyère valley in Fribouge, Switzerland. Gruyère has a mild, nutty, slightly sharp flavor that is stronger than that of American-style Swiss cheese.

Grilled Asparagus *and* Fennel Pasta Salad

Prep Time: 15 Minutes • Start to Finish: 50 Minutes • 2 servings

SALAD

- ¼ pound asparagus, cut into 2-inch pieces
- 1 medium fennel bulb, cut into thin wedges
- 1 small red onion, cut into thin wedges
- 2 teaspoons olive or vegetable oil
- ¼ teaspoon salt
- 1½ cups uncooked rainbow rotini pasta (5 ounces)
- 1 small orange, peeled and coarsely chopped

VINAIGRETTE

- 2 tablespoons olive or vegetable oil
- 2 tablespoons white balsamic vinegar
- ¼ teaspoon sugar
- ⅛ teaspoon salt

1 Heat coals or gas grill for direct heat. In medium bowl, mix asparagus, fennel, onion, oil and salt until vegetables are coated. Place in grill basket. Grill 5 to 6 inches from medium heat 10 to 15 minutes, stirring vegetables or shaking grill basket frequently, until vegetables are crisp-tender. Cool slightly.

2 While vegetables are grilling, cook and drain pasta as directed on package. Rinse with cold water; drain.

3 In small bowl, mix all vinaigrette ingredients with whisk until blended. Add cooked pasta, orange and vinaigrette to asparagus mixture in bowl; toss to mix. Serve immediately, or cover and refrigerate up to 2 hours before serving.

1 Serving: Calories 570; Total Fat 20g (Saturated Fat 3g, Trans Fat 0g); Cholesterol 0mg; Sodium 760mg; Total Carbohydrate 83g (Dietary Fiber 10g); Protein 15g **Exchanges:** 3 Starch, 1 Other Carbohydrate, 4 Vegetable, 3½ Fat **Carbohydrate Choices:** 5½

Swap It Grill any of your favorite vegetables. Try 1-inch pieces of bell peppers and sliced zucchini, yellow summer squash and mushrooms.

Swap It White wine vinegar can be used in place of the white balsamic vinegar.

Layered Salad in a Jar

Prep Time: 20 Minutes • Start to Finish: 20 Minutes • 2 servings

1 container (6 oz) fat-free lemon cream pie yogurt

1 tablespoon white balsamic or white wine vinegar

3 cups bite-size pieces romaine lettuce

1 cup chopped sweet red bell pepper

1 cup sliced celery

2 hard-cooked eggs, chopped

½ cup frozen sweet peas, cooked

¼ cup shredded fat-free Cheddar cheese (1 oz)

1 In small bowl, mix yogurt and vinegar; set aside.

2 In each of two 1-quart jars or medium bowls, place half of the lettuce. Fill each jar with layers of half of the next 5 ingredients.

3 Top each jar with half of the yogurt mixture; seal jar. Refrigerate until ready to serve. To serve, pour into serving bowl, toss to coat.

1 Serving: Calories 260; Total Fat 11g (Saturated Fat 4.5g, Trans Fat 0g); Cholesterol 205mg; Sodium 270mg; Total Carbohydrate 24g (Dietary Fiber 5g); Protein 16g **Exchanges:** ½ Starch, ½ Low-Fat Milk, 2 Vegetable, 1 Lean Meat, 1 Fat **Carbohydrate Choices:** 1½

Kitchen Tip You can prepare this salad in a jar or bowl up to a day ahead. Refrigerate until ready to serve.

Swap It You can use other vegetables in this salad, such as small broccoli florets, cauliflower or green bell pepper.

Pear and Blue Cheese Salad

Prep Time: 15 Minutes • Start to Finish: 15 Minutes • 2 servings

SALAD

- 2 cups bite-size pieces romaine lettuce
- ½ red pear, thinly sliced
- 2 tablespoons crumbled blue cheese
- 2 tablespoons coarsely chopped walnuts, toasted

VINAIGRETTE

- 2 tablespoons walnut, olive or vegetable oil
- 1½ teaspoons cider vinegar
- ¼ teaspoon Dijon mustard
- ⅛ teaspoon salt
- ⅛ teaspoon pepper
- 1 clove garlic, finely chopped

1 In medium bowl, mix all salad ingredients.

2 In tightly covered container, shake all vinaigrette ingredients until well blended. Add to salad; toss to mix.

1 Serving: Calories 240; Total Fat 21g (Saturated Fat 4g, Trans Fat 0g); Cholesterol 5mg; Sodium 290mg; Total Carbohydrate 10g (Dietary Fiber 3g); Protein 3g **Exchanges:** ½ Starch, 1 Vegetable, 4 Fat **Carbohydrate Choices:** ½

Kitchen Tip To toast walnuts, heat oven to 350°F. Bake in an ungreased shallow pan about 10 minutes, stirring occasionally, until golden brown.

Fresh Tomato and Garlic Penne

Prep Time: 20 Minutes • Start to Finish: 20 Minutes • 2 servings

1¼ cups uncooked penne pasta (about 4 oz)

1 teaspoon olive oil

1 clove garlic, finely chopped

6 medium plum (Roma) tomatoes (1 lb), coarsely chopped

1 tablespoon chopped fresh basil leaves

¼ teaspoon salt

Dash pepper

1 Cook pasta as directed on package, omitting salt and oil; drain.

2 Meanwhile, in 10-inch skillet, heat oil over medium-high heat. Add garlic; cook and stir 30 seconds. Stir in tomatoes. Cook 5 to 8 minutes, stirring frequently, until tomatoes are soft and sauce is slightly thickened.

3 Stir basil, salt and pepper into tomato mixture. Cook 1 minute. Serve over pasta.

1 Serving: Calories 300; Total Fat 3g (Saturated Fat 0g, Trans Fat 0g); Cholesterol 0mg; Sodium 160mg; Total Carbohydrate 57g (Dietary Fiber 5g); Protein 11g **Exchanges:** 3 Starch, ½ Other Carbohydrate, 1 Vegetable **Carbohydrate Choices:** 4

Thai Tofu Green Curry Bowls

Prep Time: 15 Minutes • Start to Finish: 3 Hours 30 Minutes • 2 servings (2¼ cups each)

2 tablespoons soy sauce

2 teaspoons green curry paste (from 4-oz jar)

1 teaspoon finely chopped garlic

1 teaspoon finely chopped gingerroot

½ cup coconut milk (from 13.6-oz can)

½ cup vegetable or chicken broth

8 oz firm or extra-firm tofu, cut in ¾-inch cubes

¾ cup sliced mushrooms

⅓ cup chopped onion

½ medium red bell pepper, cut into 1 x ¼-inch strips

½ cup halved snow peas or ¼ cup frozen peas

1½ cups cooked jasmine or white rice

1 tablespoon chopped fresh cilantro

Lime wedges

1 In 2-quart slow cooker, stir together soy sauce, curry paste, garlic and gingerroot. Gradually stir in coconut milk and broth. Add tofu, mushrooms, onion and bell pepper.

2 Cover; cook on High 2 to 3 hours or until vegetables are tender. Stir in snow peas. Cover; cook 15 minutes longer or until pea pods are tender.

3 Spoon rice into serving bowls; top with curry mixture. Sprinkle with cilantro; garnish with lime wedges.

1 Serving: Calories 420; Total Fat 17g (Saturated Fat 10g, Trans Fat 0g); Cholesterol 0mg; Sodium 1600mg; Total Carbohydrate 47g (Dietary Fiber 3g); Protein 19g **Exchanges:** 3 Starch, 1 Vegetable, 1 Medium-Fat Meat, 2 Fat **Carbohydrate Choices:** 3

Kitchen Tip Buying coconut milk can be confusing. For this recipe, look for cans that contain coconut and water. Avoid coconut cream, which is much thicker and higher in fat, and refrigerated coconut milk, which contains more water and possibly flavorings and sweetener. Stir the coconut milk with a whisk before using, as it separates during storage.

Kitchen Tip Tofu, or bean curd, is made from soy. The varying textures, from silken and soft to extra-firm, refer to the amount of water pressed out during production. The firmer the tofu, the less water. Using extra-firm tofu in this recipe works well because the tofu holds its shape. The slow cooking process allows the tofu to take on the flavors of the sauce.

Roasted Chick Pea Gyros

Prep Time: 20 Minutes • Start to Finish: 25 Minutes • 2 gyros

1 can (15 to 16 oz) chick peas (garbanzo beans), rinsed, drained

1 teaspoon olive oil

½ teaspoon dried oregano leaves

½ teaspoon Greek seasoning

2 flatbread wraps or pita fold breads (about 7-inch diameter)

½ cup prepared tzatziki cucumber sauce (from 8-oz container)

4 thin slices medium tomato

6 thin slices cucumber

1 thin slice red onion, separated into rings

2 tablespoons crumbled feta cheese

2 teaspoons chopped fresh Italian (flat-leaf) parsley

1 Heat oven to 400°F. Line 15 × 10 × 1-inch pan with cooking parchment paper. Pat chick peas dry with paper towels, removing any loose skins. In small bowl, stir together chick peas, oil, oregano and Greek seasoning. Spread chick peas in single layer on pan.

2 Bake 15 to 20 minutes or until lightly browned.

3 To make gyros, place each flatbread wrap on microwavable plate; cover with plastic wrap. Microwave each on High 10 to 15 seconds just to soften and warm slightly.

4 Spread 2 tablespoons tzatziki sauce on 1 side of each flatbread to within 1 inch of the edges. Spoon ⅓ cup roasted chick peas over tzatziki sauce. (Save remaining roasted chick peas for another use.)

5 Place half of tomato, cucumber, onion, feta cheese and parsley over chick peas on each flatbread wrap. Serve immediately with remaining tzatziki sauce.

1 Gyro: Calories 510; Total Fat 10g (Saturated Fat 3g, Trans Fat 0g); Cholesterol 15mg; Sodium 1230mg; Total Carbohydrate 84g (Dietary Fiber 11g); Protein 20g **Exchanges:** 4½ Starch, 1 Other Carbohydrate, ½ Vegetable, ¼ Very Lean Meat, 1½ Fat **Carbohydrate Choices:** 5½

Use It Up Tzatziki sauce is a traditional Greek yogurt—based sauce with cucumber and mint. Look for it in the refrigerated section of the deli or produce area of your supermarket. Use leftovers as a salad dressing, dip for veggies or sandwich spread.

Use It Up Use the leftover roasted chick peas in a salad or on top of a pizza.

Mushroom Ravioli with Goat Cheese Alfredo Sauce

Prep Time: 30 Minutes • Start to Finish: 40 Minutes • 2 servings

RAVIOLI

- 3 tablespoons butter
- 2 cups small mushrooms, thinly sliced (6 oz)
- 2 teaspoons finely chopped garlic
- 1 tablespoon white balsamic vinegar
- 1 tablespoon fresh thyme leaves
- ⅓ cup grated Parmesan cheese
- 12 wonton wrappers (from 14-oz package)
- 1 egg, beaten

SAUCE

- ¼ cup refrigerated Alfredo pasta sauce (from 10-oz container)
- 2 tablespoons crumbled chèvre (goat) cheese
- 2 teaspoons milk

TOPPINGS

- ¼ cup frozen peas, cooked, drained
- 2 tablespoons chopped walnuts
- ½ teaspoon fresh thyme leaves

1 In 10-inch nonstick skillet, melt butter over medium heat. Add mushrooms; cook 5 to 6 minutes or until lightly browned.

2 Add garlic, balsamic vinegar and 1 tablespoon of the thyme leaves; cook 1 minute, stirring constantly. Remove from heat. Pour into small bowl; cool 10 minutes.

3 Meanwhile, fill 4-quart Dutch oven or large saucepan with about 2 quarts water and ½ teaspoon salt; heat to boiling.

4 Line cookie sheet with cooking parchment paper. Stir Parmesan cheese into mushrooms. Spoon 1 generous tablespoon of mushroom mixture onto center of each wonton. Brush edges of wonton with egg. To enclose filling, bring two opposite corners of each wonton together over center of filling forming triangle. Press edges to seal. Place on cookie sheet. Cover with plastic wrap.

5 Slip half of the ravioli into boiling water. Boil 3 minutes or until tender (do not overcook). Use slotted spoon to lift ravioli from boiling water; place on serving plate. Repeat with remaining ravioli and place on second serving plate.

6 In small microwavable bowl, stir together Alfredo pasta sauce, chèvre cheese and milk. Microwave uncovered on High 30 seconds to 1 minute, stirring after 30 seconds, until hot.

7 Sprinkle ravioli with peas and walnuts. Drizzle with sauce. Sprinkle with ½ teaspoon of the thyme leaves.

1 Serving: Calories 640; Total Fat 43g (Saturated Fat 23g, Trans Fat 1.5g); Cholesterol 190mg; Sodium 640mg; Total Carbohydrate 41g (Dietary Fiber 3g); Protein 23g **Exchanges:** 1½ Starch, ½ Other Carbohydrate, 3 Vegetable, 1 Medium-Fat Meat, ½ High-Fat Meat, 6½ Fat **Carbohydrate Choices:** 3

Kitchen Tip Cut larger mushrooms in half or quarters before slicing. Or use petite mushrooms, if available.

Use It Up! Use leftover wonton wrappers to make wonton chips. Cut wonton wrappers diagonally in half. Place in single layer on ungreased cookie sheet. Spray with cooking spray; sprinkle with sea salt. Bake at 375°F for 8 to 10 minutes or until golden brown and crisp.

Skillet Taco Spaghetti

Prep Time: 25 Minutes • Start to Finish: 35 Minutes • 2 servings (1¼ cups each)

SPAGHETTI

- 2 teaspoons vegetable oil
- ⅓ cup chopped onion
- ¾ cup frozen soy-protein crumbles
- 2 teaspoons finely chopped garlic
- 1 cup water
- 1 cup chunky-style salsa
- 2 oz uncooked spaghetti, broken in half
- ½ teaspoon ground cumin

  Chopped cilantro, if desired

TOPPINGS

- ½ cup finely shredded Mexican blend cheese

  Chopped cilantro and sliced green onions, if desired

1 In 10-inch nonstick skillet, heat oil over medium heat. Add onion and cook, stirring occasionally, 3 minutes or until onion is tender. Add soy-protein crumbles and garlic; cook 1 minute, stirring occasionally, until heated through.

2 Stir in remaining ingredients except toppings. Heat to boiling; reduce heat. Cover and simmer 10 to 12 minutes, stirring occasionally, until pasta is tender and most of liquid has been absorbed.

3 Remove skillet from heat; sprinkle with cheese. Cover and let stand 3 minutes or until cheese melts. Sprinkle with cilantro before serving.

1 Serving: Calories 380; Total Fat 14g (Saturated Fat 6g, Trans Fat 0g); Cholesterol 25mg; Sodium 1110mg; Total Carbohydrate 41g (Dietary Fiber 4g); Protein 21g **Exchanges:** 1½ Starch, 1 Other Carbohydrate, 1½ Lean Meat, 1 High-Fat Meat **Carbohydrate Choices:** 3

Kitchen Tip For meat lovers, substitute ½ pound extra lean ground beef for the soy-protein crumbles. Cook ground beef at the same time as the onion for 5 to 7 minutes, until beef is no longer pink; stir in garlic and cook for 1 minute.

Use It Up Use remaining frozen soy-protein crumbles in place of ground beef in tacos or sloppy joes. Add them to the recipe at the point the beef is cooked.

Southwest Corn Pancakes

Prep Time: 30 Minutes • Start to Finish: 30 Minutes • About 8 pancakes

¾ cup Original Bisquick mix

¼ cup cornmeal

½ cup milk

1 egg

½ cup shredded pepper Jack cheese

½ cup frozen corn, thawed

3 tablespoons chopped green chiles, undrained (from 4.5-oz can)

¾ teaspoon chili powder

Chunky salsa, if desired

Sliced ripe olives, if desired

Guacamole, if desired

1 Brush griddle or skillet with vegetable oil. Heat griddle to 375°F or heat skillet over medium heat.

2 In large bowl, stir Bisquick mix, cornmeal, milk and egg until blended. Stir in cheese, corn, chiles and chili powder. Pour batter by slightly less than ¼ cupfuls onto hot griddle; spread slightly.

3 Cook until edges are dry. Turn; cook other sides until golden. Serve with salsa, olives and guacamole.

1 Pancake: Calories 110; Total Fat 4g (Saturated Fat 2g, Trans Fat 0g); Cholesterol 30mg; Sodium 210mg; Total Carbohydrate 14g (Dietary Fiber 1g); Protein 4g **Exchanges:** 1 Starch, ½ Fat **Carbohydrate Choices:** 1

Swap It If you don't have pepper Jack cheese, use Cheddar or Monterey Jack. Use a chopped seeded jalapeño in place of the canned green chiles.

FISH and SHELLFISH

Seafood Cakes *with* Sriracha Mayo

Prep Time: 15 Minutes • Start to Finish: 1 Hour • 2 servings

SRIRACHA MAYO

- ¼ cup mayonnaise
- 2 teaspoons Sriracha sauce

SEAFOOD CAKES

- 1 package (8 oz) refrigerated chunk-style imitation crabmeat, chopped
- 2 tablespoons frozen whole kernel corn, thawed
- 2 tablespoons finely chopped red bell pepper
- 2 tablespoons thinly sliced green onions
- 2 tablespoons mayonnaise
- ½ teaspoon Dijon mustard
- ¼ teaspoon salt
- ¼ teaspoon garlic powder
- 2 eggs, lightly beaten
- ¾ cup plain panko bread crumbs
- 1 tablespoon vegetable oil

1 In small bowl, stir together Sriracha mayo ingredients until blended. Cover and refrigerate.

2 In medium bowl, combine crabmeat, corn, bell pepper, 1 tablespoon of the green onions, 2 tablespoons mayonnaise, the mustard, salt, garlic powder and eggs; mix well. Stir in ½ cup of the bread crumbs.

3 Shape crabmeat mixture into four 3-inch rounds, pressing firmly. Place on plate; cover with plastic wrap, pressing lightly. Refrigerate at least 30 minutes.

4 Place remaining ¼ cup bread crumbs on small plate. In 10-inch nonstick skillet, heat oil over medium heat. Carefully coat both sides of seafood cakes with bread crumbs; place in skillet. Press lightly with spatula. Cook 4 to 5 minutes or until golden brown on bottom.

5 Carefully turn seafood cakes over; cook 4 to 5 minutes longer or until bottoms are golden brown and seafood cakes are thoroughly heated. Top with remaining green onions and serve with Sriracha mayo.

1 Serving: Calories 700; Total Fat 46g (Saturated Fat 8g, Trans Fat 0g); Cholesterol 240mg; Sodium 1850mg; Total Carbohydrate 43g (Dietary Fiber 0g); Protein 29g **Exchanges:** 1 Starch, 2 Other Carbohydrate, 2½ Lean Meat, 1 Medium-Fat Meat, 6½ Fat **Carbohydrate Choices:** 3

Use It Up Slice remaining red bell pepper into strips and enjoy with Sriracha mayo or ranch dressing.

Sriracha Shrimp Fried Rice

Prep Time: 30 Minutes • Start to Finish: 30 Minutes • 2 servings (1½ cups each)

2 teaspoons vegetable oil

¼ lb uncooked deveined peeled medium shrimp, tail shells removed

1 teaspoon Sriracha sauce

1 red bell pepper, sliced into thin strips, then halved

½ cup fresh sugar snap peas, cut diagonally

3 medium green onions, cut diagonally, whites and greens separated

1 teaspoon finely chopped gingerroot

1 clove garlic, finely chopped

4 teaspoons gluten-free reduced-sodium soy sauce

1 tablespoon packed brown sugar

1½ cups hot cooked white rice (made without added salt or butter)

2 tablespoons lime juice

1 tablespoon sesame seed, toasted

1 In 10-inch nonstick skillet, heat 1 teaspoon of the oil over medium-high heat. Add shrimp; cook 2 minutes without moving. Stir in Sriracha sauce; turn shrimp. Cook 1 minute longer. Spoon shrimp into small bowl; cover with foil.

2 Add remaining 1 teaspoon oil, the bell pepper, peas and whites of onions to skillet. Cook 2 to 3 minutes or until vegetables are tender, stirring constantly.

3 Add gingerroot and garlic; cook and stir about 30 seconds longer to blend flavors. Add soy sauce and brown sugar; cook 1 minute longer. Add rice; cook about 1 minute or until broken up and warmed.

4 Return shrimp to pan; cook 1 minute to combine flavors. Stir in lime juice. Top with onion greens and toasted sesame seed.

1 Serving: Calories 350; Total Fat 9g (Saturated Fat 1.5g, Trans Fat 0g); Cholesterol 85mg; Sodium 920mg; Total Carbohydrate 52g (Dietary Fiber 3g); Protein 16g **Exchanges:** 3 Other Carbohydrate, 1 Vegetable, 2 Very Lean Meat, 1½ Fat **Carbohydrate Choices:** 3½

Kitchen Tip To toast sesame seed, sprinkle in small ungreased heavy skillet. Cook over medium-low heat 5 to 7 minutes, stirring frequently, until browning begins, then stirring constantly until golden brown.

Southwest Salmon *With* Cilantro-Lime Sauce

Prep Time: 30 Minutes • Start to Finish: 30 Minutes • 2 servings

½ cup sour cream

1 tablespoon chopped fresh cilantro leaves

1 teaspoon grated lime peel

2 teaspoons lime juice

½ teaspoon honey

⅛ teaspoon salt

2 salmon fillets (6 oz each)

1 tablespoon chicken taco seasoning mix (from 0.85-oz package)

1 tablespoon vegetable oil

1 In small bowl, mix sour cream, cilantro, lime peel, lime juice, honey and salt; set aside.

2 Sprinkle salmon fillets with taco seasoning mix. In 8-inch skillet, heat oil over medium heat. Add fillets to skillet, skin-side down.

3 Cook 6 to 8 minutes or until skin is browned. Turn fillets; cook 2 to 4 minutes or until salmon flakes easily with fork. Serve salmon with sour cream mixture.

1 Serving: Calories 500; Total Fat 37g (Saturated Fat 12g, Trans Fat 0g); Cholesterol 125mg; Sodium 690mg; Total Carbohydrate 7g (Dietary Fiber 0g); Protein 35g **Exchanges:** ½ Other Carbohydrate, 5 Lean Meat, 4½ Fat **Carbohydrate Choices:** ½

Kitchen Tip If you'd like to add a little heat to the cilantro-lime sauce, add 1 teaspoon finely chopped serrano chile.

Slow-Cooker Creole Jambalaya

Prep Time: 20 Minutes • Start to Finish: 8 Hours 50 Minutes • 3 servings (1½ cups each)

2 medium stalks celery, chopped (1 cup)

4 cloves garlic, finely chopped

2 cans (14.5 oz each) diced tomatoes with green pepper and onion, undrained

½ cup chopped fully cooked smoked sausage

½ teaspoon dried thyme leaves

¼ teaspoon pepper

¼ teaspoon red pepper sauce

12 oz uncooked deveined peeled medium (26 to 30 count) shrimp, thawed if frozen, tail shells removed

⅔ cup uncooked long-grain white rice

1⅓ cups water

Celery leaves, if desired

1 In 3- to 3½-quart slow cooker, mix all ingredients except shrimp, rice and water.

2 Cover; cook on Low heat setting 7 to 8 hours or until vegetables are tender.

3 Stir in shrimp. Cover; cook on Low heat setting about 30 minutes or until shrimp turn pink. Meanwhile, cook rice in water as directed on package, omitting butter and salt. Serve jambalaya with rice. Garnish with celery leaves.

1 Serving: Calories 380; Total Fat 7g (Saturated Fat 2g, Trans Fat 0g); Cholesterol 175mg; Sodium 900mg; Total Carbohydrate 50g (Dietary Fiber 3g); Protein 30g **Exchanges:** 1½ Starch, 2 Other Carbohydrate, 3 Very Lean Meat, ½ High-Fat Meat **Carbohydrate Choices:** 3

Kitchen Tip If you're trying to increase the amount of whole grains you eat, use brown rice in place of the white rice and follow the package directions for cooking.

Smoky Gouda Tuna Casserole

Prep Time: 15 Minutes • Start to Finish: 35 Minutes • 2 servings (1¼ cups each)

1 cup uncooked penne pasta

1 cup fresh Brussels sprouts, halved (about 5 oz)

½ cup shredded smoked Gouda cheese (2 oz)

¼ cup chopped drained roasted red bell peppers (from 12-oz jar)

2 tablespoons milk

⅛ teaspoon pepper

3 oz cream cheese, cubed

1 can (5 oz) albacore tuna in water, drained

¼ cup crushed cheese crackers or spicy nacho-flavored tortilla chips

1 Heat oven to 350°F. Spray 1-quart casserole with nonstick cooking spray. In 2-quart saucepan, cook pasta as directed on package, adding Brussels sprouts during last 10 minutes of cooking; drain.

2 Return pasta and Brussels sprouts to saucepan; stir in remaining ingredients, except crushed crackers. Cook and stir over low heat until cheese is melted.

3 Spoon pasta mixture into the casserole. Sprinkle with crackers.

4 Bake 15 to 20 minutes or until hot and bubbly.

1 Serving: Calories 690; Total Fat 29g (Saturated Fat 15g, Trans Fat 1g); Cholesterol 105mg; Sodium 1080mg; Total Carbohydrate 69g (Dietary Fiber 5g); Protein 38g **Exchanges:** 3 Starch, 1 Other Carbohydrate, 1 Vegetable, 3 Lean Meat, 1 High-Fat Meat, 2 Fat **Carbohydrate Choices:** 4½

Swap It If you prefer, try substituting cooked, chopped salmon or shrimp for the tuna. You can also substitute cut asparagus or broccoli florets for the Brussels sprouts.

Swap It Try another shaped pasta, or a gluten-free variety, for the penne pasta. Be sure to use a pasta shape that is about the same size.

California Kimchi Tuna Melts

Prep Time: 10 Minutes • Start to Finish: 15 Minutes • 2 servings

2   slices (½-inch-thick) sourdough bread

1   can (5 oz) tuna in water, drained

½   cup coarsely chopped kimchi

1   tablespoon mayonnaise

1   small tomato, thinly sliced

½   avocado, thinly sliced

2   slices Cheddar cheese, cut into 4 triangles

1 Move oven rack 4 to 6 inches from broiler. Set oven control to broil. Line cookie sheet with foil. Place bread slices on cookie sheet.

2 Broil about 1 minute on each side until light brown.

3 In small bowl, stir together tuna, kimchi and mayonnaise. Spoon tuna mixture evenly over toasted bread slices. Arrange tomato and avocado slices on top of tuna. Top each with 2 triangles of cheese.

4 Broil sandwiches 2 to 3 minutes or just until cheese is melted.

1 Serving: Calories 380; Total Fat 20g (Saturated Fat 6g, Trans Fat 0g); Cholesterol 50mg; Sodium 690mg; Total Carbohydrate 23g (Dietary Fiber 4g); Protein 25g **Exchanges:** 1 Starch, 1 Vegetable, 2 Very Lean Meat, 1 High-Fat Meat, 2 Fat **Carbohydrate Choices:** 1½

Kitchen Tip Kimchi is a Korean culinary staple made from fermented vegetables (usually cabbage and radishes) and seasonings. You can find kimchi in a variety of heat levels and textures. Look for kimchi at your grocery store, farmers' market or food co-op.

Swap It You can swap out the sourdough for marbled rye, whole wheat, rye bread or Challah bread. Just be sure you use slices about the same size as sourdough so all the yummy fillings will fit on top.

Salmon Sandwiches

Prep Time: 20 Minutes • Start to Finish: 25 Minutes • 2 sandwiches

½ cup dry bread crumbs

2 teaspoons Dijon mustard

⅛ teaspoon coarse ground pepper

4 medium green onions, finely chopped (¼ cup)

1 egg, slightly beaten

1 can (7½ oz) red salmon, skin and bone removed, drained and flaked

2 teaspoons canola oil

2 tablespoons ranch dressing

2 whole wheat burger buns, split

Lettuce leaves

1 In medium bowl, mix together bread crumbs, mustard, pepper, green onions, egg and salmon. Shape mixture into 2 patties, using heaping ½ cupfuls for each patty; flatten slightly.

2 In 10-inch nonstick skillet, heat oil over medium heat. Cook patties in oil 8 to 10 minutes, turning once, until brown and cooked through.

3 Spread ranch dressing on bottom half of each bun. Top buns with lettuce and salmon patties.

1 Sandwich: Calories 510; Total Fat 23g (Saturated Fat 4g, Trans Fat 0g); Cholesterol 165mg; Sodium 1030mg; Total Carbohydrate 42g (Dietary Fiber 5g); Protein 33g **Exchanges:** 1½ Starch, 1 Other Carbohydrate, ½ Vegetable, 4 Medium-Fat Meat, ½ Fat **Carbohydrate Choices:** 3

Kitchen Tip Prepare salmon patties up to a day ahead and refrigerate; cook before serving.

Swap It Use tartar sauce or mayonnaise in place of the ranch dressing.

Cheesy Tuna-Vegetable Chowder

Prep Time: 20 Minutes • Start to Finish: 20 Minutes • 2 servings (1¼ cups each)

2 tablespoons butter

¼ cup chopped onion (1 small)

2 tablespoons all-purpose flour

¼ teaspoon ground mustard

Dash pepper

1 cup milk

½ cup chicken broth (from 32-oz carton)

1 cup frozen mixed vegetables

⅛ teaspoon dried marjoram leaves, crushed

½ cup shredded Cheddar–Monterey Jack cheese blend (2 oz)

1 can (4.5 oz) tuna, drained, flaked

1 In 2-quart saucepan, melt butter over medium heat. Add onion; cook and stir until tender. Reduce heat to low. Stir in flour, mustard and pepper; cook and stir until mixture is smooth and bubbly.

2 Gradually stir in milk and broth. Stir in frozen vegetables and marjoram. Heat to boiling over medium heat, stirring occasionally. Reduce heat to low; cover and simmer 3 to 5 minutes or until vegetables are crisp-tender.

3 Add cheese and tuna; heat, stirring gently, until cheese is melted.

1 Serving: Calories 330; Total Fat 16g (Saturated Fat 10g, Trans Fat 0.5g); Cholesterol 65mg; Sodium 610mg; Total Carbohydrate 22g (Dietary Fiber 2g); Protein 24g **Exchanges:** ½ Starch, 1 Other Carbohydrate, 3 Very Lean Meat, 3 Fat **Carbohydrate Choices:** 1½

Swap It Substitute any of your favorite shredded cheeses in this hearty chowder.

Cajun Shrimp Chowder

Prep Time: 30 Minutes • Start to Finish: 30 Minutes • 2 servings (1½ cups each)

1 slice bacon, finely chopped

1 small dark-orange sweet potato (about ½ lb), peeled, cubed (about 1½ cups)

⅓ cup chopped onion

1 teaspoon finely chopped garlic

½ teaspoon Cajun seasoning

1¼ cups chicken broth

1 cup frozen fire-roasted corn

½ lb frozen uncooked deveined peeled medium shrimp (tail shells removed)

¼ cup half-and-half

3 tablespoons thinly sliced green onions

1 In 2-quart saucepan, cook bacon over medium heat 2 to 3 minutes or until crisp. Remove from heat. Using slotted spoon, remove bacon to paper towel–lined plate; set aside.

2 Add sweet potato and onion to bacon drippings; cook 3 minutes, stirring frequently.

3 Add garlic and Cajun seasoning to sweet potato; cook 1 minute, stirring constantly. Add broth and corn. Heat to boiling; reduce heat. Simmer 8 minutes, stirring occasionally until sweet potato is almost tender.

4 Stir in shrimp and half-and-half; cover and cook 4 to 6 minutes, stirring occasionally, or just until shrimp turn pink. Spoon chowder into shallow bowls; top with bacon pieces and green onions.

1 Serving: Calories 350; Total Fat 7g (Saturated Fat 3g, Trans Fat 0g); Cholesterol 190mg; Sodium 1640mg; Total Carbohydrate 45g (Dietary Fiber 6g); Protein 26g **Exchanges:** ½ Starch, 2 Other Carbohydrate, 1½ Vegetable, 3 Very Lean Meat, 1 Fat **Carbohydrate Choices:** 3

Use It Up Purchase chicken broth in a resealable carton. The remaining broth can be stored in the refrigerator or frozen in small amounts (thaw before using) for other recipes.

Swap It Purchasing shrimp can be tricky! Shrimp size is determined by the number of individual shrimp in a pound. The smaller the number of shrimp per pound, the larger the shrimp. Medium shrimp have 36 to 50 shrimp per pound. You can use larger shrimp in this recipe, but you will have to cook it slightly longer. Cooking the shrimp until just pink will tell you when it is done.

Mixed Vegetable Clam Chowder

Prep Time: 10 Minutes • Start to Finish: 10 Minutes • 2 servings (1¼ cups each)

1 can (18.5 oz) New England clam chowder

1 cup frozen mixed vegetables, thawed

⅛ teaspoon dried thyme leaves

2 tablespoons shredded Cheddar cheese

Sour cream and cilantro leaves, if desired

1 In 2-quart saucepan, stir together all ingredients except sour cream and cilantro leaves. Cook over medium heat until hot, stirring frequently.

2 To serve, ladle chowder into bowls; garnish with sour cream and cilantro leaves.

1 Serving: Calories 270; Total Fat 13g (Saturated Fat 4g, Trans Fat 0g); Cholesterol 15mg; Sodium 1020mg; Total Carbohydrate 29g (Dietary Fiber 3g); Protein 8g **Exchanges:** 1½ Starch, 1 Vegetable, 2½ Fat **Carbohydrate Choices:** 2

Swap It Any frozen vegetables you may have in your freezer, such as corn, broccoli cuts or green beans, can be used in place of the frozen mixed vegetables.

Fish *and* Veggie Soup

Prep Time: 20 Minutes • Start to Finish: 30 Minutes • 2 servings (1¼ cups each)

1 slice bacon, finely chopped

¼ cup chopped onion

¼ cup chopped celery

½ teaspoon finely chopped garlic

¾ cup tomato juice

¾ cup clam juice (from 8-oz bottle)

½ cup sliced halved zucchini

½ cup sliced quartered summer squash

6 oz medium-firm fish fillet, such as haddock or cod, cut into 1-inch pieces

1 bay leaf

½ teaspoon seafood seasoning blend

1 tablespoon chopped fresh parsley

1 In 2-quart saucepan, cook and stir bacon over medium heat 4 to 5 minutes or until bacon begins to crisp. Stir in onion, celery and garlic. Cook and stir 3 to 4 minutes until vegetables are crisp-tender.

2 Stir in remaining ingredients except parsley. Cover; heat to boiling. Reduce heat; simmer 10 minutes or until fish flakes easily with fork and zucchini is tender.

3 Ladle into 2 soup bowls; sprinkle with parsley.

1 Serving: Calories 120; Total Fat 2.5g (Saturated Fat 0.5g, Trans Fat 0g); Cholesterol 50mg; Sodium 840mg; Total Carbohydrate 8g (Dietary Fiber 1g); Protein 17g **Exchanges:** 1½ Vegetable, 2 Very Lean Meat, ½ Fat **Carbohydrate Choices:** ½

Use It Up Adding a crunchy topping will give your taste buds a terrific treat. Use what you have on hand—croutons, oyster crackers or coarsely crushed crackers or tortilla chips.

Use It Up Buy tomato juice in a large jar or can, or in a 6-pack of cans. Each can contains 6 ounces, or ¾ cup of juice—just enough for this recipe. Use remaining juice in other soup recipes, in Bloody Marys or for a quick and healthy beverage.

Scallop *and* Bacon Tetrazzini

Prep Time: 30 Minutes • Start to Finish: 30 Minutes • 2 servings

3 oz uncooked spaghetti

4 slices thick-cut bacon, cut into ½-inch pieces

½ lb sea scallops (6 scallops)

⅛ teaspoon garlic salt

⅛ teaspoon pepper

1½ cups sliced mushrooms (4 oz)

2 tablespoons sliced green onions

½ cup half-and-half

¾ cup shredded Gruyère cheese (3 oz)

Sliced green onions, if desired

1 Cook spaghetti as directed on package; drain.

2 Meanwhile, in 10-inch skillet, cook bacon over medium heat 8 to 10 minutes, stirring occasionally, until crisp. Remove bacon with slotted spoon; drain on paper towels. Measure 2 tablespoons drippings into small, heatproof bowl; discard any remaining drippings.

3 Sprinkle scallops with garlic salt and pepper. Add 1 tablespoon of the drippings to skillet. Cook scallops in drippings over medium heat about 5 minutes, turning once, until golden brown, and white and opaque inside. Place scallops on plate.

4 Add remaining 1 tablespoon drippings to skillet. Add mushrooms and green onions; cook 2 to 3 minutes over medium heat or until mushrooms are tender. Stir in half-and-half, Gruyère cheese and cooked spaghetti; cook until cheese is melted and mixture is slightly thickened. Add scallops and bacon; cook about 1 minute. Garnish with green onions. Serve immediately.

1 Serving: Calories 620; Total Fat 30g (Saturated Fat 15g, Trans Fat 0.5g); Cholesterol 115mg; Sodium 1330mg; Total Carbohydrate 46g (Dietary Fiber 3g); Protein 42g **Exchanges:** 2 Starch, ½ Other Carbohydrate, 1 Vegetable, 2½ Very Lean Meat, 2½ High-Fat Meat, 1½ Fat **Carbohydrate Choices:** 3

Swap It Smaller bay scallops may be used in place of the larger sea scallops. Although you will use the same amount, the bay scallops will cook more quickly and will not brown like the sea scallops.

Kitchen Tip If you don't have a kitchen scale to weigh the spaghetti, tightly bundle the spaghetti with one hand and measure the pieces together to equal the width of a penny.

Kitchen Tip For a creamier sauce, you may want to add an additional tablespoon of half-and-half. We suggest serving immediately because as the pasta sits, it continues to absorb the liquid.

Thai Red Curry Shrimp Skillet

Prep Time: 30 Minutes • Start to Finish: 30 Minutes • 2 servings (1¼ cups each)

2 oz uncooked stir-fry rice noodles

1½ teaspoons vegetable oil

⅓ cup coarsely chopped red bell pepper

¼ cup diced shallots or onions

½ teaspoon finely chopped garlic

1 cup unsweetened coconut milk (from 13.66-oz can)

2 tablespoons Thai red curry paste (from 4-oz jar)

½ cup sugar snap peas, cut in half

6 oz uncooked deveined peeled medium or large shrimp, tail shells removed (about 14)

2 teaspoons fish sauce (from 6.76-oz jar)

Red pepper flakes, if desired

Chopped fresh Thai basil or regular basil, if desired

1 Cook rice noodles as directed on package; drain.

2 Meanwhile, in 10-inch nonstick skillet, heat oil over medium heat. Add pepper and shallots to skillet; cook, stirring occasionally, 3 to 4 minutes, or until vegetables are crisp-tender. Stir in garlic; cook 30 seconds.

3 Stir in coconut milk, curry paste and peas; heat to boiling. Stir in shrimp; reduce heat to low; simmer 2 to 3 minutes or until shrimp turn pink. Stir in rice noodles and fish sauce; cook 1 to 2 minutes or until heated through. Let stand 2 to 3 minutes for sauce to thicken before serving. Sprinkle with red pepper flakes. Garnish with basil.

1 Serving: Calories 450; Total Fat 25g (Saturated Fat 19g, Trans Fat 0g); Cholesterol 115mg; Sodium 840mg; Total Carbohydrate 38g (Dietary Fiber 3g); Protein 19g **Exchanges:** 1 Starch, 1 Other Carbohydrate, 1 Vegetable, 2 Very Lean Meat, 4½ Fat **Carbohydrate Choices:** 2½

Swap It Thai basil (identifiable by its purple stem) has notes of mint and citrus, which is great for Asian dishes. However, sweet basil may be substituted, if desired.

Use It Up Remaining coconut milk can be refrigerated and used to add delicious flavor to oatmeal, cereal or a fruit smoothie.

Kitchen Tip Try serving topped with chopped salted peanuts.

Swap It Frozen shrimp can be used in this recipe. Thaw before using. To thaw, place shrimp in bowl of cold water for about 15 minutes; drain.

Herbed Fish

Prep Time: 15 Minutes • Start to Finish: 15 Minutes • 2 servings

3 tablespoons seasoned dry bread crumbs

2 tablespoons all-purpose flour

2 teaspoons chopped fresh basil leaves or ½ teaspoon dried basil leaves

⅛ teaspoon salt

1 egg, slightly beaten

½ lb cod, tilapia, haddock or other mild-flavored fish fillets (about ½ inch thick)

1 tablespoon olive or vegetable oil

1 In shallow dish, stir bread crumbs, flour, basil and salt. In another shallow dish, place egg. Cut fish into 2 pieces. Dip fish into egg; coat with bread crumb mixture.

2 In 10-inch skillet, heat oil over medium heat. Reduce heat to medium-low. Add fish; cook 6 to 8 minutes, turning once, until fish flakes easily with fork and is brown on both sides.

1 Serving: Calories 250; Total Fat 9g (Saturated Fat 1.5g, Trans Fat 0g); Cholesterol 60mg; Sodium 450mg; Total Carbohydrate 15g (Dietary Fiber 0g); Protein 25g **Exchanges:** 1 Starch, 3 Lean Meat **Carbohydrate Choices:** 1

Kitchen Tip Top the fish with an easy basil sauce. Mix ¼ cup mayonnaise and 1 tablespoon chopped fresh basil. For added zest, serve with lemon wedges.

Sheet Pan Asian Salmon *with* Vegetables

Prep Time: 15 Minutes • Start to Finish: 40 Minutes • 2 servings

1 tablespoon teriyaki sauce

3 teaspoons vegetable oil

2 teaspoons Sriracha sauce

2 salmon fillets (6 oz each)

½ teaspoon toasted sesame oil

⅛ teaspoon red pepper flakes

⅛ teaspoon salt

6 broccoli spears

½ cup red onion wedges

½ yellow bell pepper, cut into ½-inch strips

½ teaspoon sesame seed

1 tablespoon sliced green onion

1 Heat oven to 400°F. In 1-gallon resealable food-storage plastic bag, combine teriyaki sauce, 1 teaspoon of the vegetable oil and the Sriracha sauce. Add salmon; seal bag. Turn bag to coat salmon. Refrigerate up to 2 hours.

2 In medium bowl, stir together remaining 2 teaspoons of the vegetable oil, the sesame oil, red pepper flakes and salt. Add vegetables; toss to coat. Arrange in single layer on 15 × 10 × 1-inch pan. Drizzle any remaining oil mixture in bowl over vegetables.

3 Bake, uncovered, 10 minutes; remove from oven.

4 Cut 12-inch square of foil; fold in half. With spatula, move vegetables to half of pan. Place foil on side of pan next to vegetables. Remove salmon from marinade, reserving marinade. Place salmon skin side down on foil. Bake vegetables and salmon, uncovered, 8 minutes; brush with some of the remaining marinade. Return to oven; bake 4 to 7 minutes longer or until fish flakes easily with fork.

5 Arrange fish and vegetables on serving platter. Sprinkle sesame seed over vegetables and green onion over salmon.

1 Serving: Calories 440; Total Fat 27g (Saturated Fat 5g, Trans Fat 0g); Cholesterol 90mg; Sodium 750mg; Total Carbohydrate 14g (Dietary Fiber 3g); Protein 36g **Exchanges:** ½ Other Carbohydrate, 2 Vegetable, 4½ Lean Meat, 2½ Fat **Carbohydrate Choices:** 1

Kitchen Tip Purchased teriyaki sauce is fairly thin and teriyaki glaze is very thick. This recipe was tested with the thinner sauce.

Swap It One cup of halved fresh Brussels sprouts can be substituted for the broccoli. Use whatever color bell pepper you have on hand.

Oven-Fried Bruschetta Fish

Prep Time: 15 Minutes • Start to Finish: 30 Minutes • 2 servings

¼ cup Italian-style panko crispy bread crumbs

2 tablespoons grated Parmesan cheese

2 cod, whitefish or other medium-firm fish fillets (½ inch thick), skin removed (4 to 5 oz each)

3 tablespoons mayonnaise

Cooking spray

½ cup pico de gallo salsa, drained

1 tablespoon thinly sliced fresh basil leaves

1 Heat oven to 400°F. Line cookie sheet with cooking parchment paper. In shallow bowl or pie plate, mix bread crumbs and Parmesan cheese.

2 With spatula or knife, spread one side of each fillet with ¾ tablespoon of the mayonnaise. Dip coated side of fillet in crumb mixture. Spread other side of each fillet with ¾ tablespoon of mayonnaise. Turn fillet over; dip in crumb mixture. Place fillets on cookie sheet. Spray top of fillets with cooking spray.

3 Bake 15 to 20 minutes or until crust is golden brown and fish flakes easily with fork.

4 Meanwhile, in small bowl, mix salsa and basil. Place baked fillets on serving plates. Top each with half the salsa mixture.

1 Serving: Calories 300; Total Fat 19g (Saturated Fat 3.5g, Trans Fat 0g); Cholesterol 55mg; Sodium 710mg; Total Carbohydrate 12g (Dietary Fiber 0g); Protein 22g **Exchanges:** ½ Starch, ½ Vegetable, 3 Very Lean Meat, 3½ Fat **Carbohydrate Choices:** 1

Kitchen Tip Pico de gallo salsa is a fresh tomato salsa made from fresh chopped tomatoes, onion, jalapeños, cilantro and lime juice. It can be found refrigerated in the deli, produce or dairy section of your local grocery store.

Halibut *and* Veggie Oven Packets

Prep Time: 25 Minutes • Start to Finish: 45 Minutes • 2 servings

½ cup water

½ cup instant brown rice (from 14-oz box)

1 cup chopped bell pepper (any color)

1 cup chopped fresh asparagus spears

1 teaspoon finely chopped garlic

¾ teaspoon chopped fresh rosemary leaves

½ teaspoon kosher (coarse) salt

¼ teaspoon coarse black pepper

½ lb halibut fillets, ½ to ¾ inch thick

¼ cup dry white wine

1 tablespoon butter

Grated lemon peel, if desired

1 Heat oven to 375°F. Cut 2 (18 × 12-inch) pieces of heavy-duty foil; spray foil with cooking spray. In 1-quart saucepan, heat water to boiling; stir in rice, bell pepper, asparagus and ½ teaspoon of the garlic. Return to boiling; reduce heat to low. Cover and simmer 5 minutes.

2 Remove saucepan from heat; let stand covered 5 minutes or until water is absorbed. Stir in ½ teaspoon of the rosemary, ¼ teaspoon of the salt and ⅛ teaspoon of the pepper.

3 Spoon rice mixture evenly onto center of each foil piece. Cut halibut into 2 pieces. Place fish on rice mixture; drizzle each with 2 tablespoons wine. Sprinkle halibut with remaining garlic, rosemary, salt and pepper. Top each fillet with 1½ teaspoons butter.

4 Bring up 2 sides of foil so edges meet. Seal edges, making tight ½-inch fold; fold again, allowing space for heat circulation and expansion. Fold other sides to seal.

5 Place packets on 15 × 10 × 1-inch pan. Bake 15 to 20 minutes or until fish flakes easily with fork and vegetables are crisp-tender. Reseal packets; let stand 5 minutes. To serve, carefully unwrap foil to allow steam to escape. Garnish with grated lemon peel.

1 Serving: Calories 280; Total Fat 8g (Saturated Fat 4g, Trans Fat 0g); Cholesterol 70mg; Sodium 420mg; Total Carbohydrate 26g (Dietary Fiber 4g); Protein 24g **Exchanges:** ½ Starch, ½ Other Carbohydrate, 2 Vegetable, 2½ Very Lean Meat, 1½ Fat **Carbohydrate Choices:** 2

Kitchen Tip
Halibut fillets vary in thickness. Be sure to select a fillet that has even thickness for best doneness results.

Swap It
See what kind of fish is on sale! You can use other fish with a firm texture, such as grouper, pompano or tuna.

Use It Up
Here's a great way to use up an open bottle of wine! Or, if you need to open a bottle and don't think you will drink the rest, purchase a small airline-size bottle.

Sesame Shrimp & Apple Salad

Prep Time: 15 Minutes • Start to Finish: 15 Minutes • 2 servings

8 uncooked deveined peeled large shrimp

Wooden skewers

4½ teaspoons cider vinegar

1 tablespoon olive oil

1 tablespoon sugar

1½ teaspoons soy sauce

¾ teaspoon toasted sesame oil

Freshly ground black pepper

3 cups baby lettuce leaves

1 small Granny Smith apple, cut into thin matchsticks

½ red bell pepper, cut into thin matchsticks

1 Heat oven to 400°F. Line cookie sheet with cooking parchment paper or foil. Thread shrimp onto skewers, 2 to 4 per skewer.

2 In small bowl, beat vinegar, olive oil, sugar, soy sauce and sesame oil with whisk until well blended. Use 1 tablespoon dressing to brush over shrimp; sprinkle with pepper.

3 Bake 5 to 8 minutes or until shrimp turn pink.

4 In large bowl, toss lettuce, apple and bell pepper with dressing. Divide salad evenly between 2 serving plates. Top each with shrimp.

1 Serving: Calories 190; Total Fat 9g (Saturated Fat 1g, Trans Fat 0g); Cholesterol 45mg; Sodium 260mg; Total Carbohydrate 21g (Dietary Fiber 3g); Protein 7g **Exchanges:** ½ Fruit, ½ Other Carbohydrate, 1½ Vegetable, ½ Lean Meat, 1½ Fat **Carbohydrate Choices:** 1½

Swap It If you don't have skewers, you can bake the shrimp by placing on baking sheet.

Kitchen Tip You can add a little zip to your salad dressing with a little Sriracha or hot sauce and sprinkle in a few sesame seeds.

BREAKFAST

Tomato-Topped Canadian Bacon *and* Cheese Frittata

Prep Time: 10 Minutes • Start to Finish: 25 Minutes • 2 servings

4   eggs

2   tablespoons milk

¼   teaspoon pepper

2   oz chopped Canadian bacon (⅓ cup)

¼   cup shredded sharp Cheddar cheese

1½   teaspoons olive oil

¼   cup chopped shallots or onion

1¼   cups fresh spinach leaves, chopped

½   cup chopped tomatoes

1 Heat oven to 400°F. In medium bowl, beat eggs, milk and pepper with whisk just until blended; stir in Canadian bacon and cheese; set aside.

2 In 8-inch ovenproof nonstick skillet, heat 1 teaspoon of the oil over medium heat. Add shallots; cook 1 to 2 minutes or until tender. Add 1 cup of the spinach, stirring constantly, just until it begins to wilt.

3 Pour egg mixture into skillet; cook 1 to 2 minutes or until edges are set. Carefully place skillet in oven; bake 6 to 8 minutes or until knife inserted in center comes out clean. Let stand 5 minutes.

4 Meanwhile, in small bowl, combine remaining ¼ cup spinach, the tomatoes and remaining ½ teaspoon olive oil. To serve, cut frittata into wedges; top with tomato mixture.

1 Serving: Calories 310; Total Fat 20g (Saturated Fat 7g, Trans Fat 0g); Cholesterol 405mg; Sodium 470mg; Total Carbohydrate 9g (Dietary Fiber 1g); Protein 24g **Exchanges:** 2 Vegetable, 1 Lean Meat, 2 Medium-Fat Meat, 1½ Fat **Carbohydrate Choices:** ½

Use It Up Leftover spinach can be used to make a fresh spinach salad. Toss with some basil pesto, tomatoes and feta cheese for a great side salad.

Swap It Use fresh salsa as an alternative topping to the spinach and tomato mixture.

Cheese Omelets

Prep Time: 5 Minutes • Start to Finish: 10 Minutes • 2 servings

4 eggs

4 teaspoons butter

½ cup shredded Cheddar cheese (2 oz)

Salt and pepper, if desired

1 For each omelet, beat 2 eggs in small bowl with fork or whisk until yolks and whites are well blended.

2 In 8-inch skillet, heat 2 teaspoons of the butter over medium-high heat until melted. As butter melts, tilt skillet to coat bottom with butter.

3 Quickly pour eggs into skillet. While rapidly sliding skillet back and forth over heat, quickly stir eggs with fork to spread them continuously over the bottom of the skillet as they thicken. When they are thickened, let stand over heat a few seconds to lightly brown bottom of omelet. Do not overcook; omelet will continue to cook after being folded. Sprinkle with cheese.

4 Tilt skillet and run spatula under edge of omelet to loosen from bottom of skillet. Fold portion of omelet nearest you just to center. Allow for a portion of omelet to slide up side of skillet. Slide omelet onto warm plate, flipping folded portion of omelet over so far side is on bottom. Tuck sides of omelet under, if desired. Sprinkle with salt and pepper.

1 Serving: Calories 330; Total Fat 28g (Saturated Fat 13g, Trans Fat 0.5g); Cholesterol 420mg; Sodium 370mg; Total Carbohydrate 2g (Dietary Fiber 0g); Protein 19g **Exchanges:** 2 Medium-Fat Meat, ½ High-Fat Meat, 3 Fat **Carbohydrate Choices:** 0

Swap It Use Monterey Jack, Swiss or crumbled blue cheese instead of the Cheddar if you like.

Basil-Vegetable Scramble

Prep Time: 10 Minutes • Start to Finish: 20 Minutes • 2 servings

2   cups cubed cooked potatoes (2 medium)

1   small onion, chopped (¼ cup)

¼   cup chopped red bell pepper

4   eggs

1   tablespoon chopped fresh basil leaves or 1 teaspoon dried basil leaves

¼   teaspoon salt

⅛   teaspoon ground red pepper (cayenne)

1 Spray 10-inch skillet with cooking spray; heat over medium heat. Cook potatoes, onion and bell pepper in skillet about 5 minutes, stirring occasionally, until hot.

2 Beat remaining ingredients until well blended; pour into skillet. As mixture begins to set at bottom and side, gently lift cooked portions with spatula so that thin, uncooked portion can flow to bottom. Avoid constant stirring. Cook 2 to 4 minutes or until eggs are cooked but still moist.

1 Serving: Calories 290; Total Fat 11g (Saturated Fat 3.5g, Trans Fat 0g); Cholesterol 375mg; Sodium 430mg; Total Carbohydrate 32g (Dietary Fiber 2g); Protein 15g **Exchanges:** 2 Other Carbohydrate, 1 Vegetable, 2 Medium-Fat Meat **Carbohydrate Choices:** 2

Kitchen Tip The trick to fluffy, moist scrambled eggs is avoiding constant stirring and carefully lifting the cooked portions with a spatula.

Swap It You can substitute ½ cup frozen stir-fry bell peppers and onions for the chopped onion and bell pepper.

Weekend Breakfast Egg Sandwiches

Prep Time: 15 Minutes • Start to Finish: 15 Minutes • 2 sandwiches

2 tablespoons butter, softened

2 pretzel buns (4 inch diameter), sliced in half horizontally

2 eggs

2 slices (¾ oz each) Cheddar cheese

¾ cup shredded coleslaw mix (from 14-oz bag)

2 tablespoons red pepper jelly

⅔ cup refrigerated shredded pork in barbecue sauce (from 16-oz container)

1 Heat 10-inch nonstick skillet over medium heat. Spread butter over cut sides of buns. Place 2 bun halves cut side down in skillet. Cook 1 to 2 minutes or until golden brown. Remove from skillet. Repeat with remaining bun halves. Reduce heat to low.

2 Break 1 of the eggs into custard cup or small bowl; slip into skillet. Repeat with remaining egg. Cook covered 5 to 7 minutes until whites and yolks are firm, not runny. Remove pan from heat. Place cheese slice on each egg. Cover pan; let stand 1 minute or until cheese is melted.

3 Meanwhile, in small bowl, mix coleslaw mix with red pepper jelly. In microwavable small bowl, place shredded pork; cover with microwavable plastic wrap. Microwave on High 1 to 2 minutes until hot, stirring halfway through cooking.

4 Place half of hot pork mixture on bottom of each bun. Top each with cheese-topped egg and half of coleslaw mixture. Place toasted bun tops on top of the coleslaw mixture. Serve immediately.

1 Sandwich: Calories 600; Total Fat 36g (Saturated Fat 17g, Trans Fat 1g); Cholesterol 275mg; Sodium 710mg; Total Carbohydrate 42g (Dietary Fiber 1g); Protein 26g **Exchanges:** 1½ Starch, 1 Other Carbohydrate, ½ Vegetable, 1 Lean Meat, 1 Medium-Fat Meat, 1 High-Fat Meat, 4 Fat **Carbohydrate Choices:** 3

Swap It Pretzel buns aren't the only delicious way to make this sandwich. Try it with bagels, kaiser rolls or onion buns.

Swap It Leftover barbecued beef or chicken can be substituted for the shredded pork in barbecue sauce.

Use It Up Peach jam, apricot preserves, apple jelly or other jams or preserves you might have in your refrigerator can be used in place of the red pepper jelly. Add a little zing to the jam with a dash of red pepper sauce.

Southwestern Breakfast Tostadas

Prep Time: 10 Minutes • Start to Finish: 20 Minutes • 2 servings

- 2 corn tortillas (6 inch)
- ½ cup black beans (from 15-oz can), rinsed, drained
- ½ cup fat-free egg product
- 1 tablespoon fat-free (skim) milk
- ⅛ teaspoon pepper
  Dash salt
- ½ cup chopped tomato
- 2 tablespoons crumbled queso fresco or shredded Monterey Jack cheese
- 2 teaspoons chopped fresh cilantro
- 2 tablespoons fat-free Greek yogurt

1 Warm tortillas as directed on package. Meanwhile, in small bowl, use potato masher or fork to slightly mash beans; set aside.

2 In another small bowl or 1-cup glass measure, combine egg, milk, pepper and salt. Beat with whisk until well blended.

3 Heat 10-inch nonstick skillet over medium heat. Pour egg mixture into skillet. Cook, without stirring, until egg mixture begins to set. Run spatula around edge of skillet, lifting egg mixture so that uncooked portion flows underneath. Continue cooking about 2 minutes more or until egg mixture is cooked but still moist. Remove from heat.

4 Spread 1 of the tortillas with mashed beans. Top with remaining tortilla, cooked egg mixture, tomato, cheese and 1 teaspoon of the cilantro. Cut in half to serve. If desired, fold each portion in half. Top with yogurt and remaining 1 teaspoon cilantro.

1 Serving: Calories 190; Total Fat 3g (Saturated Fat 1g, Trans Fat 0g); Cholesterol 5mg; Sodium 440mg; Total Carbohydrate 26g (Dietary Fiber 7g); Protein 15g **Exchanges:** 1½ Starch, 1½ Very Lean Meat, ½ Fat **Carbohydrate Choices:** 2

Use It Up Leftover yogurt mixed with a little honey and cinnamon makes a delicious spread for bagels or toast.

Huevos Rancheros Quesadillas

Prep Time: 25 Minutes • Start to Finish: 25 Minutes • 2 servings

½ cup fat-free egg product
or 2 eggs

1 tablespoon water

Dash salt

¼ teaspoon chili powder

2 medium green onions,
sliced (2 tablespoons)

4 soft white corn tortillas
(6 inch)

¼ cup fat-free refried beans

2 tablespoons chunky-
style salsa

¼ cup shredded reduced-fat
sharp Cheddar cheese
(1 oz)

Reduced-fat sour cream,
if desired

Additional salsa, if desired

1 In small bowl, beat egg product, water, salt and chili powder with whisk until blended.

2 Heat 10-inch nonstick skillet over medium heat. Add onions; cook 1 to 2 minutes or until crisp-tender. Reduce heat to medium-low. Add egg mixture; cook 2 to 3 minutes, stirring frequently, until eggs are set but still moist. Remove from skillet; keep warm.

3 Spread each of 2 tortillas with 2 tablespoons refried beans and 1 tablespoon salsa. Top with egg mixture, cheese and remaining tortillas.

4 Wipe out skillet. Heat over medium heat. Cook each quesadilla in skillet 3 minutes, turning carefully halfway through cooking, until crisp. Cut each quesadilla into quarters. Serve with sour cream and additional salsa.

1 Serving: Calories 190; Total Fat 2.5g (Saturated Fat 1g, Trans Fat 0g); Cholesterol 0mg; Sodium 590mg; Total Carbohydrate 28g (Dietary Fiber 4g); Protein 14g **Exchanges:** 2 Starch, 1 Very Lean Meat **Carbohydrate Choices:** 2

Shakshuka

Prep Time: 15 Minutes • Start to Finish: 25 Minutes • 2 servings

2 teaspoons olive oil

⅓ cup chopped onion

⅓ cup chopped red
bell pepper

½ teaspoon finely chopped
garlic

1 can (14 to 15 oz)
fire-roasted diced
tomatoes

2 tablespoons chopped
fresh Italian (flat-leaf)
parsley

¾ teaspoon ground cumin

¾ teaspoon paprika

¼ teaspoon sugar

¼ teaspoon salt

¼ teaspoon crushed red
pepper flakes

2 eggs

1 tablespoon crumbled
feta cheese

Crusty white bread,
if desired

1 Heat oven to 375°F. In 8-inch ovenproof skillet, combine oil, onion, bell pepper and garlic; cook over medium heat 3 minutes, stirring constantly until onion is softened.

2 Stir in tomatoes, 1 tablespoon of the parsley, the cumin, paprika, sugar, salt and crushed red pepper; heat to boiling. Reduce heat; simmer 5 minutes or until slightly thickened.

3 With back of spoon, make 2 (3-inch) indentations in tomato mixture. Break eggs, one at a time, into custard cup; carefully slide egg into each indentation. Bake, uncovered, 9 to 12 minutes or until whites are firm but yolks are still slightly runny. Bake longer, if desired, for firm yolks. Sprinkle with remaining 1 tablespoon parsley and the feta cheese. Serve with bread.

1 Serving: Calories 200; Total Fat 11g (Saturated Fat 3g, Trans Fat 0g); Cholesterol 190mg; Sodium 710mg; Total Carbohydrate 16g (Dietary Fiber 3g); Protein 9g **Exchanges:** ½ Other Carbohydrate, 2 Vegetable, 1 Medium-Fat Meat, 1 Fat **Carbohydrate Choices:** 1

Kitchen Tip This dish hails from North Africa and the Middle East. Each region has a slightly different version, but whatever the combination, this tomato and egg dish makes a lovely brunch dish or an easy weeknight dinner.

Swap It If you have shredded Parmesan, Romano or crumbled goat cheese, you can use that instead of the feta.

Individual Hoagie Stratas

Prep Time: 15 Minutes • Start to Finish: 40 Minutes • 2 hoagie stratas

1 hoagie bun (7 to 8 inches)

4 eggs

1 tablespoon milk

¼ teaspoon salt

⅛ teaspoon pepper

2 slices Canadian bacon, diced (about 1 oz)

⅓ cup ½-inch pieces fresh asparagus

2 oz Brie cheese, cubed

1 Heat oven to 350°F. Line cookie sheet with cooking parchment paper. Cut hoagie bun in half horizontally. Using fingers, remove interior of bread leaving about ½-inch shell. Coarsely tear bread from center of hoagie; set aside. Place bread halves on cookie sheet, cut side up.

2 In medium bowl, beat eggs with whisk. Beat in milk, salt and pepper until well blended. Stir in reserved torn bread and remaining ingredients. Carefully spoon mixture equally between bread halves.

3 Bake, uncovered, 18 to 20 minutes or until eggs are set. Let stand 5 minutes before serving.

1 Hoagie Strata: Calories 420; Total Fat 21g (Saturated Fat 9g, Trans Fat 0g); Cholesterol 410mg; Sodium 980mg; Total Carbohydrate 29g (Dietary Fiber 1g); Protein 27g **Exchanges:** 2 Starch, 2½ Medium-Fat Meat, ½ High-Fat Meat, ½ Fat **Carbohydrate Choices:** 2

Swap It Lots of chances to customize this easy meal! Use other cheeses instead of the Brie, like Camembert or Havarti. If you prefer it meatless, omit the Canadian bacon and add a little extra asparagus. You can also substitute cooked ham, bacon or sausage for the Canadian bacon.

Kitchen Tip Brie cheese is a soft cheese and will be easier to cut when cold, so refrigerate or place in the freezer for a few minutes before cutting. The rind on Brie cheese is typically eaten, so no need to remove it before cutting into cubes.

Bacon *and* Egg Naan Pizzas

Prep Time: 10 Minutes • Start to Finish: 30 Minutes • 2 pizzas

1   tablespoon butter, melted

⅛   teaspoon garlic powder

2   oval-shaped Tandoori naan flatbreads (9 × 5-inch)

¾   cup shredded Cheddar and mozzarella cheese blend

½   cup cooked chopped applewood smoked bacon (6 slices)

4   eggs

1   teaspoon chopped fresh chives

     Sriracha sauce, if desired

1 Heat oven to 375°F. Line cookie sheet with cooking parchment paper. In small bowl, mix butter and garlic powder. Place naan flatbreads on cookie sheet; brush with butter mixture. Sprinkle with ½ cup of the cheese and ¼ cup of the bacon on outside edge of each flatbread.

2 Break 1 of the eggs into a small custard cup. Carefully pour egg into center of 1 flatbread. Repeat with second egg; place next to egg on flatbread. Repeat with the second flatbread and remaining 2 eggs. Sprinkle remaining bacon around the eggs.

3 Bake, uncovered, 15 minutes. Remove from oven; top with remaining ¼ cup cheese. Bake an additional 3 to 5 minutes or until whites and yolks are firm and cheese is melted. Sprinkle with chives and drizzle with Sriracha sauce.

1 Pizza: Calories 1140; Total Fat 67g (Saturated Fat 34g, Trans Fat 1.5g); Cholesterol 530mg; Sodium 1660mg; Total Carbohydrate 81g (Dietary Fiber 3g); Protein 54g **Exchanges:** 2 Medium-Fat Meat **Carbohydrate Choices:** 5½

Swap It Regular bacon may be swapped for the applewood smoked bacon.

Use It Up Naan flatbread may be frozen for later use. It's traditionally served as a side bread with Indian dishes but is great for making individual pizzas.

Kitchen Tip Naan flatbread often has 1 side that has more of a lip than the other side. Use the side with the lip up to hold the eggs in the center.

Apple, Cheddar *and* Sausage Sandwiches

Prep Time: 25 Minutes • Start to Finish: 25 Minutes • 2 sandwiches

8   oz bulk pork sausage

1   tablespoon vegetable oil

2   eggs
    Salt and pepper, if desired

¼   cup apple butter

4   slices (½ inch thick) Italian bread

½   cup shredded sharp Cheddar cheese (2 oz)

2   tablespoons butter, softened

1 Heat 12-inch nonstick skillet over medium heat. Divide sausage in half and shape into flat patties slightly bigger than the diameter of each bread slice. Place patties in hot skillet; cook about 8 minutes, turning once, until pork is no longer pink in center. Drain on paper towel–lined plate. Remove drippings from skillet and wipe out with paper towel.

2 In same skillet, heat oil over medium heat until hot. Break each egg into skillet and sprinkle with salt and pepper. Cook until whites of eggs are set. Turn eggs over. Use tip of spatula to pierce each yolk. Cook eggs 1 minute or until yolks are set. Remove eggs from skillet and place directly on top of sausage patties on paper towels.

3 Spread 2 tablespoons of the apple butter on 1 side of 2 bread slices. Top each slice with sausage and egg. Sprinkle each with ¼ cup cheese. Cover with remaining bread slices. Spread half of butter over top slices of bread.

4 In same skillet, place sandwiches butter sides down. Spread remaining butter over top slices of bread. Cook, uncovered, over medium heat about 5 minutes or until bottoms are golden brown. With spatula, carefully turn sandwiches over. Cook 2 to 3 minutes longer or until bottoms are golden brown and cheese is melted. Serve hot.

1 Sandwich: Calories 680; Total Fat 49g (Saturated Fat 20g, Trans Fat 1g); Cholesterol 290mg; Sodium 990mg; Total Carbohydrate 33g (Dietary Fiber 2g); Protein 26g **Exchanges:** 2 Starch, 3 High-Fat Meat, 5 Fat **Carbohydrate Choices:** 2

Swap It For convenience, purchase pre-formed sausage patties and cook as directed in recipe.

Florentine Eggs on English Muffins

Prep Time: 15 Minutes • Start to Finish: 15 Minutes • 2 servings

¼ cup plain fat-free Greek yogurt (from 6-oz container)

1 tablespoon reduced-fat mayonnaise

½ teaspoon Dijon mustard

2 eggs

1 English muffin, split, toasted

½ cup fresh baby spinach leaves

2 slices tomato

Dash pepper

1 In small microwavable bowl, mix yogurt, mayonnaise and mustard. Microwave uncovered on High 20 to 40 seconds or until warm. Stir; cover to keep warm.

2 In 10-inch skillet, heat 2 to 3 inches water to boiling. Reduce heat to medium-low so water is simmering. Break 1 cold egg into custard cup or small glass bowl. Holding cup close to water's surface, carefully slide egg into water. Repeat with second egg. Quickly spoon hot water over each egg until film forms over yolk. Cook, uncovered, 3 to 5 minutes or until whites and yolks are firm, not runny.

3 Meanwhile, spread about 2 tablespoons sauce on each muffin half. Top each with half of the spinach and 1 tomato slice.

4 With slotted spoon, remove eggs from water; place over tomato. Top with remaining sauce; sprinkle with pepper.

1 Serving: Calories 180; Total Fat 8g (Saturated Fat 2.5g, Trans Fat 0g); Cholesterol 190mg; Sodium 260mg; Total Carbohydrate 16g (Dietary Fiber 1g); Protein 11g **Exchanges:** 1 Starch, 1 Medium-Fat Meat, ½ Fat **Carbohydrate Choices:** 1

Use Up What You Have

Sometimes it's not possible to purchase a small quantity of an ingredient when cooking for one or two. Fear not! This chart will show you which recipes share an ingredient as well as other clever ways to use them up. If you don't see the ingredient in the main recipe, check the tips for how to use it. See Ingredients Storage Chart, page 164, for how to store perishable ingredients.

LEFTOVER INGREDIENT	RECIPES THAT USE IT	OTHER USES FOR LEFTOVERS
Bacon	BLT Poutine (page 294) Blue Cheese and Bacon Twice-Baked Potatoes (page 286) Cajun Shrimp Chowder (page 198) Cheddar-Bacon Corn Muffins with Chipotle Butter (page 281) Fish and Veggie Soup (page 203) Individual Hoagie Stratas (page 232) Pimiento Cheese and Corn–Stuffed Mini Peppers (page 273)	Add to eggs, salads, stir into mashed potatoes or to top casseroles.
Barbecued beef, prepared	Barbecued Beef Shepherd's Pie (page 102) Weekend Breakfast Egg Sandwiches (page 224)	Top baked potatoes, use in tacos, quesadillas.
Basil, fresh	Basil-Vegetable Scramble (page 223) Cheesy Cauliflower Crusted Rosemary and Tomato Pizza (page 143) Chicken Sausage and Bean Soup (page 24) Oven-Fried Bruschetta Fish (page 212) Polenta and Spinach–Stuffed Tomatoes (page 154) White Bean Hummus (page 271)	Add it finely sliced or chopped to salads, cooked veggies or mashed sweet or regular potatoes. Place a leaf or two in a pitcher of water with a few slices of lemon or strawberries for a delicious flavored water.
Bell pepper	Chicken Tomato Curry with Coconut Quinoa (page 50) Chutney Potato Salad (page 296) Sheet Pan Asian Salmon with Vegetables (page 211) Southern Hot Corn (page 306) Thai Tofu Green Curry Bowls (page 173) Seafood Cakes with Sriracha Mayo (page 185) White Bean Hummus (page 271)	Add chopped to salads, egg dishes or casseroles. Eat fresh with dip for a snack.
Chicken broth	Buffalo Chicken Chili (page 20) Butternut Squash and Leek Stuffing (page 301) Cajun Shrimp Chowder (page 198) Cheesy Potato Soup (page 158) Cheesy Tuna-Vegetable Chowder (page 197) Chicken Sausage and Bean Soup (page 24) Chicken Tortilla Soup (page 22) Creamy Southwestern Corn Chowder (page 161) Ham and Cheese–Stuffed Pork Chops with Dijon Sauce (page 120) Creamy Smothered Ranch Pork Chops (page 123) North Woods Wild Rice Soup (page 27) One-Pot Creamy Chicken Spaghetti (page 47) Orange Chicken with Snow Peas and Carrots (page 54) Slow-Cooker Chicken in Red Wine (page 64) Slow-Cooker Creamy Herbed Chicken Stew (page 29) Spicy Pork Carnitas Soup (page 134) Thai Tofu Green Curry Bowls (page 173) White Bean Hummus (page 271)	Thin very thick soups, mashed potatoes or chiles; simmer with veggies for a quick soup.

LEFTOVER INGREDIENT	RECIPES THAT USE IT	OTHER USES FOR LEFTOVERS
Chicken thighs	Chicken Tomato Curry with Coconut Quinoa (page 50) Indian-Spiced Chicken, Cauliflower and Peas (page 62) Slow-Cooker Chicken in Red Wine (page 64) Slow-Cooker Creamy Herbed Chicken Stew (page 29) Slow-Cooker Mexican Chicken Tostadas (page 19) Spicy Pork Carnitas Soup (page 134)	Use in most recipes calling for boneless, skinless chicken breast halves, strips or pieces.
Cilantro	Banh Mi Pizza Panini (page 12) Black Bean–Stuffed Sweet Potatoes (page 156) Chicken Tomato Curry with Coconut Quinoa (page 50) Chicken Tortilla Soup (page 22) Indian-Spiced Chicken, Cauliflower and Peas (page 62) Quick Dinner Nachos (page 144) Skillet Taco Spaghetti (page 178) Southwestern Breakfast Tostadas (page 226) Southwest Salmon with Cilantro-Lime Sauce (page 188) Spicy Barbecue Chicken Flatbread Pizza (page 274) Spicy Pork Carnitas Soup (page 134) Spinach–White Bean Enchiladas (page 148) Thai Tofu Green Curry Bowls (page 173)	Chop with garlic clove to stir into softened butter, for a savory spread. Top casseroles, egg or Mexican dishes. Chop and stir into dips.
Coconut	Chocolate and Toasted Coconut Yogurt Bowls (page 256) Coconut Cream Pie Bites (page 329) Glazed Lemon-Coconut Bars (page 319) Tropical Smoothie Bowls (page 253)	Stir into drop cookie dough, pancake batter or brownie batter. Add to fruit salads or sprinkle over ice cream.
Coconut milk	Chicken Tomato Curry with Coconut Quinoa (page 50) Thai Red Curry Shrimp Skillet (page 206) Thai Tofu Green Curry Bowls (page 173)	Add to smoothies or as part of the liquid when making rice.

Continued from previous page

LEFTOVER INGREDIENT	RECIPES THAT USE IT	OTHER USES FOR LEFTOVERS
Coleslaw mix	Weekend Breakfast Egg Sandwiches (page 224)	Add to green or fruit salads or soups.
Corn, frozen whole kernel	Barbecued Beef Shepherd's Pie (page 102) Cajun Shrimp Chowder (page 198)	Add to eggs, Mexican dishes or salads.
Cream cheese	Carrot Cake with Cream Cheese Frosting (page 326) Impossibly Easy Mocha Fudge Cheesecakes (page 334) Pimiento Cheese and Corn-Stuffed Mini Peppers (page 273) Smoky Gouda Tuna Casserole (page 193)	Top with salsa or jam and serve with crackers for a snack or stir into mashed potatoes.
Ginger, crystallized	Ginger, Walnut and White Chocolate Cookies (page 311) Whole-Grain Raspberry French Toast (page 243)	Steep in hot water for tea, stir into muffin or pancake batter, add to cookie dough, sprinkle over ice cream.
Egg yolk	Cinnamon-Frosted Molasses Cookies (page 314) Coconut Cream Pie Bites (page 329) Giant Peanut Butter and Candy Cookie (page 313) Ginger, Walnut and White Chocolate Cookies (page 311)	Add to eggs while cooking, use to make puddings and custards.
Frozen peas	Chutney Potato Salad (page 296) Indian-Spiced Chicken, Cauliflower and Peas (page 62) Mushroom Ravioli with Goat Cheese Alfredo Sauce (page 176) Thai Tofu Green Curry Bowls (page 173)	Add cooked, cooled peas to tuna, egg, macaroni or green salads. Add cooked to pasta dishes or stir-fries.
Green chiles, canned	Barbecued Beef Shepherd's Pie (page 102) Southern Hot Corn (page 306) Southwest Corn Pancakes (page 181) Spicy Chicken Enchiladas (page 43) Spicy Pork Carnitas Soup (page 134) Spinach–White Bean Enchiladas (page 148)	Add to egg or Mexican dishes, soups, chilies or salads.

LEFTOVER INGREDIENT	RECIPES THAT USE IT	OTHER USES FOR LEFTOVERS
Ground beef, lean	Ancho Chili Beef Soup (page 87) Beef and Vegetable Stir-Fry (page 91) Black and Blue Mini Meat Loaves (page 82) Curried Beef Pizzas (page 92) Easy Beef Enchiladas (page 79) Slow-Cooker Couscous-Stuffed Peppers (page 147) Teriyaki Beef–Stuffed Peppers (page 84)	Use to make burgers or quick skillet meals with veggies. Add to soups, chilies.
Plain yogurt	Banana Bread Muffins (page 279) Chutney Potato Salad (page 296) Florentine Eggs on English Muffins (page 237) Gluten-Free Buffalo Chicken Salad (page 35) Indian-Spiced Chicken, Cauliflower and Peas (page 62) Peanut Butter–Banana Smoothie Bowls (page 251) Southwestern Breakfast Tostadas (page 226)	Use in place of sour cream on Mexican dishes, baked potatoes.
Rosemary, fresh	Cheesy Cauliflower Crusted Rosemary and Tomato Pizza (page 143) Small Batch No-Knead Rosemary-Parmesan Bread (page 282) Sheet Pan Turkey Dinner (page 39) Veggie Burgers with Caramelized Onions (page 153)	Add to potato or rice dishes, to season meat or poultry.
Semisweet chocolate chips	Chocolate–Peanut Butter Lava Cakes (page 322) Ice-Cream Sandwich Bites (page 347) Triple Chocolate Skillet Brownie Sundae (page 316)	Stir into ice cream, add to muffin or pancake batter.
Shrimp	Cajun Shrimp Chowder (page 198) Sesame Shrimp and Apple Salad (page 217) Slow-Cooker Creole Jambalaya (page 191) Smoky Gouda Tuna Casserole (page 193) Sriracha Shrimp Fried Rice (page 186) Thai Red Curry Shrimp Skillet (page 206)	Serve cold with cocktail sauce for a quick appetizer, add to egg dishes, soups or substitute for tuna in tuna salad.
Sour cream	Banana Bread Muffins (page 279) Blue Cheese and Bacon Twice-Baked Potatoes (page 286) Browned Butter Mashed Potatoes (page 289) Chicken and Corn Quesadillas (page 44) Curried Beef Pizzas (page 92) Salted Caramel–Pecan Cheesecake (page 332) Spicy Chicken Enchiladas (page 43)	Use it in place of plain yogurt in recipes calling for plain yogurt. Stir into mashed potatoes, to top Mexican dishes.
Squash, butternut	Butternut Squash and Leek Stuffing (page 301) Vegetarian Tostadas (page 151)	Roast as a veggie side dish, add to skillet meals or casseroles. Add to vegetable salads.
Thyme, fresh	Halibut and Veggie Oven Packets (page 214) Mushroom Ravioli with Goat Cheese Alfredo Sauce (page 176) Sausage and Wild Mushroom Skillet Pizza (page 136)	Add to mushroom or veggie dishes, egg dishes or as a seasoning for meat, poultry or fish.
Tomato paste	Indian-Spiced Chicken, Cauliflower and Peas (page 62) Hungarian Beef Goulash with Sour Cream Dumplings (page 101)	Add to tomato-based soups, chili.
Vegetable broth	Polenta and Spinach–Stuffed Tomatoes (page 154) Thai Tofu Green Curry Bowls (page 173) White Bean Hummus (page 271)	Use in place of chicken broth—reduce salt in recipes as the dishes will be saltier.

Whole-Grain Raspberry French Toast

Prep Time: 20 Minutes • Start to Finish: 20 Minutes • 2 servings

TOPPING

3   tablespoons raspberry
    fruit spread

1   cup frozen
    organic raspberries

1   tablespoon finely chopped
    crystallized ginger or
    ¼ teaspoon ground ginger

FRENCH TOAST

½   cup fat-free egg product
    or 2 eggs

¼   cup fat-free (skim) milk

2   teaspoons sugar

1   teaspoon vanilla

¼   teaspoon ground
    cinnamon

3   slices white whole-
    grain bread, each cut in
    half diagonally

1 In small saucepan, heat fruit spread and raspberries over low heat until warm, stirring occasionally. Remove from heat. Stir in ginger.

2 In shallow bowl, beat egg product, milk, sugar, vanilla and cinnamon with whisk until blended.

3 Spray griddle or 10-inch skillet with cooking spray; heat griddle to 375°F or heat skillet over medium heat. Dip each slice of bread into egg mixture, turning to coat both sides; let stand in egg mixture to soak 30 to 60 seconds. Place on griddle; cook 4 to 6 minutes, turning once, until golden brown on both sides. Top each serving with fruit spread mixture.

1 Serving: Calories 310; Total Fat 2g (Saturated Fat 0g, Trans Fat 0g); Cholesterol 0mg; Sodium 320mg; Total Carbohydrate 59g (Dietary Fiber 12g); Protein 13g **Exchanges:** 2 Starch, ½ Fruit, 1½ Other Carbohydrate, 1 Very Lean Meat **Carbohydrate Choices:** 4

Fruity Pancake Tacos

Prep Time: 5 Minutes • Start to Finish: 10 Minutes • 2 servings

4 small cooked buttermilk pancakes, cooled to room temperature

1 container (4 oz) whipped strawberry yogurt

½ cup fresh fruit (such as sliced strawberries, blueberries and raspberries)

1 Place pancakes on plate; fold up sides of each to make taco shape.

2 Spoon about 2 tablespoons yogurt into each pancake taco. Top with fruit. Serve immediately.

1 Serving: Calories 230; Total Fat 2.5g (Saturated Fat 1g, Trans Fat 0g); Cholesterol 5mg; Sodium 460mg; Total Carbohydrate 45g (Dietary Fiber 2g); Protein 6g **Exchanges:** 2 Starch, ½ Fruit, ½ Other Carbohydrate, ½ Fat **Carbohydrate Choices:** 3

Swap It Swap chocolate chip pancakes for buttermilk pancakes, if desired.

Cinnamon Dutch Babies

Prep Time: 15 Minutes • Start to Finish: 40 Minutes • 2 servings

CINNAMON DUTCH BABIES

- ¼ cup all-purpose flour
- 1 tablespoon sugar
- ¼ teaspoon ground cinnamon
- ¼ teaspoon salt
- 1 egg plus 2 egg whites
- ¼ cup warm milk (105°F to 115°F)

TOPPINGS

- ¼ cup whipping cream
- 1 tablespoon salted caramel ice-cream topping
- Powdered sugar, if desired
- 1 cup fresh berries (such as blackberries, blueberries and raspberries)

1 Heat oven to 400°F. Place two 5½- to 6-inch pie plates or shallow casserole dishes on 12½x9½x1-inch pan. Place pan with pie plates in oven for 5 minutes.

2 Meanwhile, in small bowl, combine flour, sugar, cinnamon and salt until blended. In medium bowl, beat egg and egg whites with whisk until well combined. Beat in milk. Add flour mixture; mix well. (Mixture may be slightly lumpy.)

3 Remove pan with pie plates from oven. Spray pie plates with cooking spray. Immediately pour batter evenly into hot pie plates. Return to oven.

4 Bake 18 to 20 minutes or until puffy and deep golden brown. Reduce oven temperature to 300°F (do not open oven door). Bake an additional 5 minutes.

5 Meanwhile, in small bowl, beat whipping cream until soft peaks form. Beat in caramel topping until blended.

6 Immediately sprinkle Dutch babies with powdered sugar. Spoon whipped cream and berries into Dutch babies. Serve immediately.

1 Serving: Calories 310; Total Fat 13g (Saturated Fat 7g, Trans Fat 0g); Cholesterol 130mg; Sodium 440mg; Total Carbohydrate 36g (Dietary Fiber 3g); Protein 11g **Exchanges:** 1 Starch, 1 Fruit, ½ Other Carbohydrate, 1 Medium-Fat Meat, 1½ Fat **Carbohydrate Choices:** 2½

Swap It Fruit such as sliced fresh peaches, strawberries or bananas can be used in place of the berries.

Kitchen Tip A Dutch baby is also known as a German pancake. They are very easy to make! Each step in the recipe is important, though, for success. The pie dishes are heated ahead and the milk warmed to help the Dutch babies puff before the crusts set. Also, don't be surprised when the Dutch babies fall back into the dishes as they are removed from the oven. This is completely normal.

Blueberry Maple Overnight Oatmeal

Prep Time: 5 Minutes • Start to Finish: 8 Hours 5 Minutes • 2 servings

½ cup milk

2 containers (5.3 oz each) Greek vanilla or blueberry yogurt

1 cup quick-cooking oats

2 to 3 teaspoons maple-flavored syrup

½ cup fresh blueberries

¼ cup chopped pecans, toasted, if desired

Additional fresh blueberries, if desired

1 In container with tight-fitting cover, mix milk, yogurt, oats and maple syrup. Stir in ½ cup blueberries. Cover and refrigerate overnight.

2 Just before serving, top with toasted pecans and extra blueberries.

1 Serving: Calories 360; Total Fat 4g (Saturated Fat 1g, Trans Fat 0g); Cholesterol 5mg; Sodium 80mg; Total Carbohydrate 62g (Dietary Fiber 5g); Protein 18g **Exchanges:** 2 Starch, 1½ Other Carbohydrate, 1 Skim Milk, ½ Very Lean Meat **Carbohydrate Choices:** 4

Swap It What mood are you in today? Use kiwifruit, strawberries, raspberries or even sliced grapes.

Kitchen Tip To toast pecans, sprinkle in ungreased heavy skillet. Cook over medium heat 5 to 7 minutes, stirring frequently, until pecans begin to brown, then stirring constantly until pecans are light brown.

Peanut Butter–Banana Smoothie Bowls

Prep Time: 10 Minutes • Start to Finish: 10 Minutes • 2 servings

SMOOTHIES

- 1 cup plain Greek yogurt
- 2 cups frozen banana slices (2 medium)
- ¼ cup creamy peanut butter
- 2 tablespoons real maple syrup

TOPPINGS

- ½ cup honey, almond and chia granola
- 1 medium banana, sliced
- 2 tablespoons peanut butter, melted
- 1 tablespoon shaved dark chocolate

1 In blender, combine yogurt, frozen banana slices, ¼ cup peanut butter and the maple syrup. Cover and blend on high speed until smooth, stopping blender to push down mixture or scrape sides as needed.

2 Pour into 2 serving bowls. Top each serving with toppings. Serve immediately.

1 Serving: Calories 760; Total Fat 34g (Saturated Fat 8g, Trans Fat 0g); Cholesterol 10mg; Sodium 300mg; Total Carbohydrate 87g (Dietary Fiber 9g); Protein 27g **Exchanges:** 1 Starch, 1½ Fruit, 3 Other Carbohydrate, ½ Low-Fat Milk, 3 High-Fat Meat, 1½ Fat **Carbohydrate Choices:** 6

Swap It Try this recipe with any granola that you like.

Tropical Smoothie Bowls

Prep Time: 10 Minutes • Start to Finish: 10 Minutes • 2 servings

SMOOTHIES

1   container (6 oz) piña colada, mango or pineapple yogurt

1   cup chopped fresh pineapple

1   cup chopped frozen mango

¼   cup pineapple juice

TOPPINGS, IF DESIRED

1   small banana, sliced

¼   cup chopped fresh strawberries

2   tablespoons whole cashews

¼   to ½ teaspoon chia seed

2   teaspoons flaked coconut

1 In blender, place yogurt, pineapple, mango and pineapple juice. Cover and blend until smooth.

2 Pour into 2 serving bowls. Top with desired toppings.

1 Serving: Calories 300; Total Fat 6g (Saturated Fat 2g, Trans Fat 0g); Cholesterol 5mg; Sodium 55mg; Total Carbohydrate 56g (Dietary Fiber 4g); Protein 6g **Exchanges:** 1½ Fruit, 2 Other Carbohydrate, ½ Skim Milk, 1 Fat **Carbohydrate Choices:** 4

Swap It Substitute fresh mango for fresh pineapple or frozen pineapple for frozen mango, if desired.

Muesli–Greek Yogurt Smoothie Bowls

Prep Time: 5 Minutes • Start to Finish: 5 Minutes • 2 servings

1   cup frozen strawberries

1   banana

1   cup Greek vanilla yogurt
    (from 32-oz container)

½   cup toasted oats muesli

1   cup fresh berries

1 In blender, combine frozen strawberries, banana and yogurt. Cover and blend on high speed until smooth.

2 Pour into 2 serving bowls; top with muesli and fresh berries.

1 Serving: Calories 310; Total Fat 4g (Saturated Fat 1g, Trans Fat 0g); Cholesterol 0mg; Sodium 90mg; Total Carbohydrate 58g (Dietary Fiber 8g); Protein 11g **Exchanges:** 1 Starch, 2½ Fruit, ½ Skim Milk, ½ Very Lean Meat, ½ Fat **Carbohydrate Choices:** 4

Swap It Any yogurt can be substituted in this recipe. If using plain Greek yogurt, add 1 to 2 teaspoons honey or maple syrup, as desired.

Swap It Ground flaxseed, chia seed and/or nuts can be added to this recipe for variety.

Chocolate *and* Toasted Coconut Yogurt Bowls

Prep Time: 10 Minutes • Start to Finish: 10 Minutes • 2 servings

2   containers (5.3 oz each) Greek vanilla yogurt

1   cup oats and dark chocolate protein granola

1   cup fresh blueberries

¼   cup shredded coconut, toasted

1 Divide yogurt, granola and berries between 2 serving bowls.

2 Top each with toasted coconut.

1 Serving: Calories 420; Total Fat 9g (Saturated Fat 5g, Trans Fat 0g); Cholesterol 0mg; Sodium 230mg; Total Carbohydrate 58g (Dietary Fiber 4g); Protein 26g **Exchanges:** 2 Starch, ½ Fruit, 1½ Skim Milk, 1 Very Lean Meat, 1 Fat **Carbohydrate Choices:** 4

Kitchen Tip To toast coconut, sprinkle in ungreased heavy skillet. Cook over medium-low heat 6 to 14 minutes, stirring frequently until browning begins, then stirring constantly until golden brown.

Pancakes for Two

Prep Time: 10 Minutes • Start to Finish: 15 Minutes • 6 pancakes

1 cup Original Bisquick mix
½ cup milk
1 egg

1 Heat skillet over medium-high heat or electric griddle to 375°F; grease with cooking spray, vegetable oil or shortening. (Surface is ready when a few drops of water sprinkled on it dance and disappear.)

2 Stir all ingredients until blended. Pour by slightly less than ¼ cupfuls onto hot griddle.

3 Cook until edges are dry. Turn; cook until golden.

1 Pancake: Calories 100; Total Fat 3g (Saturated Fat 1g, Trans Fat 0g); Cholesterol 35mg; Sodium 210mg; Total Carbohydrate 15g (Dietary Fiber 0g); Protein 3g **Exchanges:** 1 Starch, ½ Fat **Carbohydrate Choices:** 1

Swap It When you want a special breakfast for two, stir ½ cup berries into the batter and top pancakes with whipped cream.

Kitchen Tip For uniformly shaped pancakes, pour the batter from an ice-cream scoop or ¼-cup measure.

Banana-Oat-Honey Smoothies

Prep Time: 5 Minutes • Start to Finish: 5 Minutes • 2 servings (1½ cups each)

2   medium bananas, frozen

1   cup milk

¼   cup old-fashioned oats

2   containers (5.3 oz each) 100-calorie honey Greek yogurt

1 In blender, place ingredients. Cover; blend on high speed about 10 seconds or until smooth.

2 Pour into 2 glasses. Serve immediately.

1 Serving: Calories 310; Total Fat 3.5g (Saturated Fat 2g, Trans Fat 0g); Cholesterol 10mg; Sodium 140mg; Total Carbohydrate 52g (Dietary Fiber 4g); Protein 18g **Exchanges:** ½ Starch, 1½ Fruit, 1 Skim Milk, ½ Low-Fat Milk, ½ Very Lean Meat **Carbohydrate Choices:** 3½

Kitchen Tip Nutritious smoothies are quick and easy to grab on your way out the door. If you keep ripe bananas in the freezer, you'll always be ready for this refreshing shake.

Blueberry Pomegranate Smoothies

Prep Time: 5 Minutes • Start to Finish: 5 Minutes • 2 servings (¾ cup each)

1 cup fresh or frozen (do not thaw) blueberries

½ cup pomegranate juice

½ cup soymilk

Additional berries, if desired

1 In blender, place all ingredients except additional berries. Cover; blend on high speed about 1 minute or until smooth.

2 Pour into 2 glasses; serve immediately. Garnish with additional berries.

1 Serving: Calories 140; Total Fat 2g (Saturated Fat 0g, Trans Fat 0g); Cholesterol 0mg; Sodium 40mg; Total Carbohydrate 28g (Dietary Fiber 4g); Protein 3g **Exchanges:** 1 Starch, 1 Fruit **Carbohydrate Choices:** 2

Kitchen Tip If you use fresh blueberries, do not wash them until you're ready to use them.

Strawberry–Key Lime Smoothies

Prep Time: 10 Minutes • Start to Finish: 10 Minutes • 2 servings

1   cup frozen unsweetened whole strawberries

½   cup calcium-enriched orange juice or fat-free (skim) milk

2   containers (6 oz each) Key lime pie fat-free yogurt

1 In blender, place all ingredients. Cover; blend on high speed about 1 minute or until smooth.

2 Pour into 2 glasses. Serve immediately.

1 Serving: Calories 160; Total Fat 0g (Saturated Fat 0g, Trans Fat 0g); Cholesterol 0mg; Sodium 85mg; Total Carbohydrate 33g (Dietary Fiber 2g); Protein 6g **Exchanges:** ½ Starch, 1 Fruit, ½ Other Carbohydrate, ½ Skim Milk **Carbohydrate Choices:** 2

Kitchen Tip When you use frozen fruit to make a smoothie, ice usually isn't necessary, as the frozen fruit will make it cold.

Swap It Substitute cranberry or peach juice for the orange juice.

Creamy Peach Smoothies

Prep Time: 10 Minutes • Start to Finish: 10 Minutes • 3 servings

1   cup frozen sliced peaches (from 10-oz bag)

1   banana, thickly sliced

1½ cups orange juice

1   tablespoon honey

1   container (6 oz) French vanilla low-fat yogurt

Mint leaves and orange peel pieces, if desired

1 In blender or food processor, place peaches, banana, orange juice and honey. Cover; blend on high speed about 1 minute or until smooth and creamy.

2 Pour about ¼ cup mixture into each of 3 glasses; add 1 tablespoon yogurt to each. Repeat layers 2 more times. Swirl yogurt into peach mixture with knife. Garnish with mint leaves and orange peel. Serve immediately.

1 Serving: Calories 200; Total Fat 1g (Saturated Fat 0g, Trans Fat 0g); Cholesterol 0mg; Sodium 35mg; Total Carbohydrate 44g (Dietary Fiber 2g); Protein 3g **Exchanges:** 1 Starch, 2 Fruit **Carbohydrate Choices:** 3

Kitchen Tip If your blender doesn't handle frozen fruit very well, thaw the peaches slightly before adding them to the blender.

Swap It Instead of swirling the yogurt into the drink, you can add the yogurt to the other ingredients in the blender and blend everything together.

Cinnamon Cereal Smoothies

Prep Time: 5 Minutes • Start to Finish: 5 Minutes • 2 servings

½ cup cinnamon-flavored bite-size squares oven-toasted rice cereal

1 cup fat-free (skim) milk

1 container (6 oz) thick-and-creamy cinnamon roll or French vanilla yogurt

Additional cereal and ground cinnamon, if desired

1 In blender, place all ingredients except additional cereal and cinnamon. Cover; blend on high speed about 30 seconds or until smooth, stopping blender once to scrape sides.

2 Pour into 2 glasses; garnish with additional cereal and cinnamon. Serve immediately.

1 Serving: Calories 170; Total Fat 2.5g (Saturated Fat 1g, Trans Fat 0g); Cholesterol 5mg; Sodium 140mg; Total Carbohydrate 31g (Dietary Fiber 0g); Protein 7g **Exchanges:** 1½ Other Carbohydrate, 1 Skim Milk **Carbohydrate Choices:** 2

APPETIZERS
and
SIDES

RIGHT-SIZE RECIPES

White Bean Hummus

Prep Time: 20 Minutes • Start to Finish: 20 Minutes • 4 servings (¼ cup each)

1 can (15 oz) navy beans, rinsed, drained

⅓ cup chicken or vegetable broth

¼ teaspoon salt

¼ teaspoon pepper

1 teaspoon finely chopped garlic

⅓ cup shredded zucchini

2 tablespoons finely chopped red bell pepper

2 tablespoons olive oil

1 tablespoon chopped fresh basil leaves

Crostini or fresh vegetable sticks, if desired

1 In 1-quart saucepan, combine beans, chicken broth, salt, pepper and garlic; cook, uncovered, over medium heat about 10 minutes or until mixture begins to thicken. Using potato masher or fork, mash beans. Cook, uncovered, an additional 1 to 3 minutes or until thickened. Stir in remaining ingredients, except crostini.

2 Serve warm or refrigerate 1 to 2 hours to serve chilled. Serve with crostini or vegetable sticks.

1 Serving: Calories 170; Total Fat 7g (Saturated Fat 1g, Trans Fat 0g); Cholesterol 0mg; Sodium 500mg; Total Carbohydrate 20g (Dietary Fiber 8g); Protein 6g **Exchanges:** ½ Starch, 1 Other Carbohydrate, ½ Very Lean Meat, 1½ Fat **Carbohydrate Choices:** 1

Swap It There are lots of custom options for this dip. Use a flavored olive oil, like basil or garlic-flavored olive oil. We've used navy beans, but you can also use great northern or cannellini (white kidney beans). Finally, serve with warm pita bread or pita chips or your favorite crackers.

Kitchen Tip Make it a sandwich! Spread pita halves or your favorite hearty bread with the hummus and top with fresh greens, tomato slices and/or bell pepper strips.

Pimiento Cheese *and* Corn-Stuffed Mini Peppers

Prep Time: 15 Minutes • Start to Finish: 15 Minutes • 2 servings

3 miniature sweet peppers, about 3 inches long

1 oz cream cheese, softened

¼ cup shredded Cheddar cheese

¼ cup frozen whole kernel corn, cooked

2 tablespoons diced pimiento, well drained

1 tablespoon mayonnaise

¼ teaspoon red pepper sauce or Sriracha sauce

2 teaspoons crisply cooked, crumbled bacon

2 teaspoons chopped green onion

1 Cut each pepper in half lengthwise, leaving stems intact. Remove and discard seeds and membranes.

2 In small bowl, mix cream cheese, Cheddar cheese, corn, pimiento, mayonnaise and red pepper sauce until well blended.

3 Spoon a generous tablespoon of cheese mixture into each pepper half to fill. Top each with bacon and green onion. Serve immediately or store in refrigerator.

1 Serving: Calories 220; Total Fat 16g (Saturated Fat 7g, Trans Fat 0g); Cholesterol 35mg; Sodium 350mg; Total Carbohydrate 12g (Dietary Fiber 3g); Protein 6g **Exchanges:** ½ Other Carbohydrate, 1 Vegetable, ½ High-Fat Meat, 2½ Fat **Carbohydrate Choices:** 1

Use It Up Mini peppers can vary in length from 1½ to 3 inches. If you have extra filling after filling your peppers, use what's left to fill additional peppers or serve it on top of crackers, cucumber slices or as a filling for a grilled cheese sandwich.

Kitchen Tip Easy appetizer or quick snack, this recipe can be made the day before. Store covered in the refrigerator up to 24 hours before serving.

Spicy Barbecue Chicken Flatbread Pizza

Prep Time: 15 Minutes • Start to Finish: 30 Minutes • 2 servings

1 rectangular thin pizza crust or flatbread (from 10.2-oz package)

½ cup chopped cooked chicken

2 tablespoons plus 1½ teaspoons spicy barbecue sauce

½ cup shredded Monterey Jack cheese

7 green bell pepper strips (1½ × ¼ inches each)

7 red onion strips (1½ × ¼ inches each)

1 medium green onion, thinly sliced (1 tablespoon)

Chopped fresh cilantro

1 Heat oven to 375°F. Place pizza crust on ungreased cookie sheet. In small bowl, combine chicken, 2 tablespoons of the barbecue sauce and ¼ cup of the cheese. Spread chicken mixture evenly onto flatbread to within ¼ inch of edge. Top with bell pepper and red onion. Sprinkle with remaining ¼ cup shredded cheese.

2 Bake 10 to 15 minutes or until topping is heated through and cheese is melted. Remove from oven. Top with green onion; drizzle with remaining 1½ teaspoons barbecue sauce. Sprinkle with cilantro. Cut into wedges to serve.

1 Serving: Calories 280; Total Fat 12g (Saturated Fat 6g, Trans Fat 0g); Cholesterol 55mg; Sodium 630mg; Total Carbohydrate 23g (Dietary Fiber 1g); Protein 20g **Exchanges:** ½ Starch, 1 Other Carbohydrate, ½ Vegetable, 1½ Lean Meat, 1 High-Fat Meat **Carbohydrate Choices:** 1½

Swap It Feel free to use your favorite barbecue sauce if you prefer a nonspicy variety.

Use It Up Use leftover cooked chicken for this flatbread, and you have an easy appetizer that comes together quickly!

Kitchen Tip Drizzling barbecue sauce is made easy by transferring to a small food-safe storage bag, snipping a small corner from one end and squeezing to drizzle on top of flatbread.

Glazed Mini Key Lime—Cherry Scones

Prep Time: 10 Minutes • Start to Finish: 25 Minutes • 4 scones

SCONES

½ cup all-purpose flour

2 teaspoons granulated sugar

½ teaspoon baking powder

½ teaspoon grated Key lime zest

Dash salt

1 tablespoon cold butter

1 tablespoon chopped dried cherries

2 to 3 tablespoons milk

1 teaspoon butter, melted

GLAZE

2 tablespoons powdered sugar

½ to 1 teaspoon Key lime juice

Grated Key lime zest

1 Heat oven to 400°F. In small bowl, stir together flour, sugar, baking powder, ½ teaspoon lime zest and salt. Cut in cold butter with pastry blender or fork until mixture looks like coarse crumbs. Stir in cherries and enough milk, 1 tablespoon at a time, until dough leaves side of bowl and forms a ball.

2 On lightly floured surface, knead dough 5 times. Pat into 4-inch round on ungreased cookie sheet. Cut into 4 wedges; separate slightly. Brush tops of scones with melted butter.

3 Bake 9 to 11 minutes or until bottoms are golden brown.

4 Meanwhile, in small bowl, stir together powdered sugar and enough lime juice to make spreadable glaze. Spread glaze over scones; sprinkle with lime zest. Serve warm.

1 Scone: Calories 130; Total Fat 4g (Saturated Fat 2.5g, Trans Fat 0g); Cholesterol 10mg; Sodium 170mg; Total Carbohydrate 20g (Dietary Fiber 0g); Protein 2g **Exchanges:** 1 Starch, ½ Other Carbohydrate, ½ Fat **Carbohydrate Choices:** 1

Kitchen Tip If cherries seem hard and dry, plump fruit by soaking in hot water about 1 minute; drain before using.

Swap It Use other dried fruit, such as cranberries, raisins, blueberries or snipped apricots instead of the cherries.

Swap It Regular lime zest and juice can be substituted for the Key limes.

Banana Bread Muffins

Prep Time: 15 Minutes • Start to Finish: 45 Minutes • 4 muffins

½ cup all-purpose flour

¼ cup sugar

¼ teaspoon baking soda

⅛ teaspoon salt

1 medium ripe banana

2 tablespoons vegetable oil

1 tablespoon sour cream

½ teaspoon vanilla

1 egg

1 Heat oven to 350°F. Line 4 regular-size muffin cups with paper baking cups. In medium bowl, stir together flour, sugar, baking soda and salt.

2 Peel banana; mash about two-thirds of the banana to equal ¼ cup. Slice remaining banana into 8 thin slices.

3 In small bowl, beat ¼ cup mashed banana, the oil, sour cream, vanilla and egg. Stir into flour mixture all at once just until flour is moistened (batter will be lumpy). Divide evenly into paper-lined cups. Place 2 slices of banana on top of batter in each cup.

4 Bake 25 to 30 minutes or until golden brown and toothpick inserted in center comes out clean.

1 Muffin: Calories 220; Total Fat 9g (Saturated Fat 2g, Trans Fat 0g); Cholesterol 50mg; Sodium 170mg; Total Carbohydrate 32g (Dietary Fiber 1g); Protein 3g **Exchanges:** 1 Starch, 1 Other Carbohydrate, 1½ Fat **Carbohydrate Choices:** 2

Swap It If you don't have sour cream, substitute vanilla or plain yogurt.

Kitchen Tip For variety, stir into the batter 2 tablespoons chopped nuts or mini chocolate chips.

Cheddar-Bacon Corn Muffins *with* Chipotle Butter

Prep Time: 10 Minutes • Start to Finish: 30 Minutes • 4 muffins

MUFFINS

- ⅓ cup all-purpose flour
- ⅓ cup cornmeal
- 2 teaspoons sugar
- 1 teaspoon baking powder
- ¼ teaspoon salt
- ¼ cup finely shredded sharp Cheddar cheese
- 2 slices bacon, cooked, crumbled
- ⅓ cup milk
- 2 tablespoons vegetable oil
- 1 egg white, lightly beaten

BUTTER

- 2 tablespoons butter, softened
- 2 teaspoons honey
- ⅛ teaspoon ground chipotle chile

1 Heat oven to 400°F. Spray 4 regular-size muffin cups with cooking spray. In small bowl, stir together flour, cornmeal, sugar, baking powder and salt.

2 Stir in cheese and bacon. Add milk, oil and egg white; stir just until moistened. Divide batter evenly among baking cups.

3 Bake 10 to 13 minutes or until toothpick inserted in center comes out clean. Remove from pan to cooling rack.

4 Meanwhile, stir together butter, honey and chile. Serve with warm muffins.

1 Muffin: Calories 280; Total Fat 17g (Saturated Fat 7g, Trans Fat 0g); Cholesterol 30mg; Sodium 450mg; Total Carbohydrate 25g (Dietary Fiber 1g); Protein 6g **Exchanges:** 1 Starch, ½ Other Carbohydrate, ½ High-Fat Meat, 2½ Fat **Carbohydrate Choices:** 1½

Swap It Substitute chile powder for the ground chipotle chile for a milder, less smoky flavor.

Small Batch No-Knead Rosemary-Parmesan Bread

Prep Time: 20 Minutes • Start to Finish: 2 Hours 10 Minutes • 4 servings

1 to 1¼ **cups all-purpose flour**

¾ **teaspoon sugar**

½ **teaspoon regular active dry yeast**

¼ **teaspoon salt**

6 **tablespoons warm water (105°F to 115°F)**

6 **teaspoons olive oil**

3 **tablespoons grated Parmesan cheese**

1 **tablespoon chopped fresh rosemary leaves**

2 **teaspoons finely chopped garlic**

1 In large bowl, mix ½ cup of the flour, the sugar, yeast and salt. Stir in water and 4½ teaspoons of the olive oil until well mixed. Beat 2 minutes with wooden spoon.

2 Stir in ½ cup of the remaining flour, 2 tablespoons of the Parmesan cheese, 2 teaspoons of the rosemary and the garlic.

3 Stir in additional flour, 1 tablespoon at a time as needed, until dough leaves side of bowl, flour is incorporated and dough is not sticky. Cover with plastic wrap; let rise in a warm place until doubled in size, about 1 hour.

4 Line cookie sheet with cooking parchment paper. With floured hands, shape dough into a 5-inch round disk. Place on cookie sheet. Spray a piece of plastic wrap with cooking spray. Place sprayed-side-down over dough. Let rise in warm place, about 30 to 45 minutes or until dough almost doubles in size.

5 Heat oven to 400°F. Remove plastic wrap. Carefully brush top of loaf with ½ teaspoon olive oil.

6 Bake 15 minutes. Remove from oven. Brush loaf with ½ teaspoon olive oil. Sprinkle top of loaf with remaining 1 tablespoon Parmesan cheese and 1 teaspoon of the rosemary. Drizzle remaining ½ teaspoon olive oil over the cheese. Return to oven; bake an additional 5 to 8 minutes or until golden brown. Serve warm cut into wedges.

1 Serving: Calories 200; Total Fat 8g (Saturated Fat 2g, Trans Fat 0g); Cholesterol 0mg; Sodium 220mg; Total Carbohydrate 26g (Dietary Fiber 1g); Protein 5g **Exchanges:** 1½ Starch, 1½ Fat **Carbohydrate Choices:** 2

Kitchen Tip Serve this delicious side bread with olive oil mixed with chopped herbs to dip it in. Yum!

Kitchen Tip You can tell your dough has risen by using your finger to make a small dent in the dough on the side of the loaf. If the dent remains, the bread is ready to bake.

Biscuits for Two

Prep Time: 5 Minutes • Start to Finish: 15 Minutes • 5 biscuits

1¼ cups Original Bisquick mix
½ cup milk

1 Heat oven to 450°F. In medium bowl, stir Bisquick mix and milk until soft dough forms.

2 Turn dough onto surface sprinkled with Bisquick mix; knead dough 10 times. Roll ½ inch thick. Cut with 2½-inch round cutter. Place dough rounds on ungreased cookie sheet.

3 Bake 8 to 10 minutes or until golden brown.

1 Biscuit: Calories 130; Total Fat 2.5g (Saturated Fat 1g, Trans Fat 0g); Cholesterol 0mg; Sodium 300mg; Total Carbohydrate 22g (Dietary Fiber 0g); Protein 3g **Exchanges:** 1 Starch, ½ Other Carbohydrate, ½ Fat **Carbohydrate Choices:** 1½

Swap It There's no need to knead. Make drop biscuits! Stir together Bisquick mix and milk until soft dough forms; drop by spoonfuls onto ungreased cookie sheet.

Use It Up You may have a couple of biscuits left over. Use them for breakfast or lunch the next day to make sandwiches

Broccoli with Pine Nuts

Prep Time: 5 Minutes • Start to Finish: 20 Minutes • 2 servings

¾ **pound broccoli, cut into spears**

¼ **cup butter**

½ **cup pine nuts**

1 In 2-quart saucepan, heat 1 cup water to boiling; add broccoli. Cook about 10 minutes or until stems are crisp-tender; drain.

2 In 8-inch skillet, melt butter over medium heat. Cook pine nuts in butter 4 to 5 minutes, stirring frequently, until golden brown. Stir pine nuts into broccoli.

1 Serving: Calories 510; Total Fat 44g (Saturated Fat 18g, Trans Fat 1g); Cholesterol 60mg; Sodium 260mg; Total Carbohydrate 18g (Dietary Fiber 8g); Protein 9g **Exchanges:** 3 Vegetable, ½ Medium-Fat Meat, 8½ Fat **Carbohydrate Choices:** 1

Use It Up Leftover Broccoli with Pine Nuts makes a great topper for baked potatoes. You could also toss leftovers with cooked spaghetti noodles and freshly grated Parmesan cheese for a meatless main dish.

Blue Cheese *and* Bacon Twice-Baked Potatoes

Prep Time: 10 Minutes • Start to Finish: 1 Hour 30 Minutes • 2 servings

2 large unpeeled Idaho or russet baking potatoes (about 8 oz each)

¼ cup buttermilk

1 tablespoon butter, melted

⅛ teaspoon salt

Dash pepper

¼ cup crumbled blue cheese (1 oz)

2 tablespoons sliced green onions (2 medium)

4 slices thick-sliced bacon, cooked and coarsely chopped

Additional sliced green onion, if desired

Additional crumbled blue cheese

1 Heat oven to 400°F. Pierce potatoes several times with a fork to allow steam to escape during baking.

2 Bake 1 hour or until potatoes are tender when pierced in center with fork. Reduce oven temperature to 350°F.

3 When potatoes are cool enough to handle, cut thin slice from top of each potato; discard. Scoop pulp into medium bowl, leaving shells intact. Mash potatoes with potato masher or electric mixer on low speed until no lumps remain. Add buttermilk in small amounts, beating after each addition with potato masher or electric mixer on low speed.

4 Add butter, salt and pepper; beat until potatoes are light and fluffy. Stir in blue cheese, 2 tablespoons sliced green onions and bacon. Fill potato shells with mashed potato mixture, slightly mounding mixture on top. Place in 8-inch square pan. Bake about 20 minutes or until thoroughly heated. Sprinkle with additional green onion and blue cheese.

1 Serving: Calories 490; Total Fat 17g (Saturated Fat 9g, Trans Fat 0g); Cholesterol 45mg; Sodium 720mg; Total Carbohydrate 66g (Dietary Fiber 7g); Protein 18g **Exchanges:** 4½ Starch, ½ High-Fat Meat, 2 Fat **Carbohydrate Choices:** 4½

Swap It If you like, substitute Cheddar cheese for the blue cheese and sour cream or half-and-half for the buttermilk.

Kitchen Tip If you have larger potatoes, bake time may be slightly longer.

Browned Butter Mashed Potatoes

Prep Time: 30 Minutes • Start to Finish: 30 Minutes • 3 servings (⅔ cup each)

1   lb Yukon Gold potatoes, peeled, cubed

2   teaspoons finely chopped garlic

½   teaspoon salt

3   tablespoons butter (do not use margarine)

¼   cup sour cream

1   tablespoon chopped fresh chives

⅛   teaspoon pepper

2 to 4   tablespoons milk, warmed

1 In 2-quart saucepan, place potatoes, ¼ teaspoon of the salt, the garlic and enough water to just cover potatoes. Cover; heat to boiling. Reduce heat to low; simmer 8 to 10 minutes or until potatoes are fork-tender. Drain; shake pan with potatoes over low heat to remove excess moisture.

2 Meanwhile, in 1-quart saucepan, heat butter over medium heat, stirring constantly, 3 to 4 minutes or just until light brown; immediately remove from heat. Reserve 1 teaspoon of the browned butter; set aside.

3 Mash potatoes in pan with potato masher or mixer until no lumps remain. Stir in remaining browned butter, the sour cream, chives, remaining ¼ teaspoon salt and the pepper. Add milk in small amounts, mashing or beating vigorously after each addition until potatoes are light and fluffy. Spoon into serving dish; drizzle with reserved 1 teaspoon browned butter.

1 Serving: Calories 270; Total Fat 16g (Saturated Fat 9g, Trans Fat 0.5g); Cholesterol 45mg; Sodium 500mg; Total Carbohydrate 29g (Dietary Fiber 2g); Protein 3g **Exchanges:** ½ Starch, 1½ Other Carbohydrate, ½ Vegetable, 3 Fat **Carbohydrate Choices:** 2

Swap It Use what you have on hand instead of the sour cream. Try any dairy potato topper, French onion or your favorite flavor sour cream dip.

Kitchen Tip Be careful not to let the butter burn or it will taste bitter. If you have a saucepan with a dark bottom, it may be difficult to see the difference between browned butter and burnt butter. Try spooning a little butter onto a white or clear plate to see the color more clearly.

Kitchen Tip Shaking the potatoes in the pan removes excess moisture to make the fluffiest potatoes.

Deluxe Au Gratin Potato Wedges

Prep Time: 20 Minutes • Start to Finish: 1 Hour 15 Minutes • 2 servings

1 tablespoon butter

4 teaspoons all-purpose flour

¼ teaspoon salt

¼ teaspoon dry mustard

⅛ teaspoon pepper

¾ cup milk

⅓ cup shredded Gruyère cheese

2 to 3 medium red potatoes, each cut lengthwise into 8 wedges (8 oz)

1 tablespoon chopped fresh chives

1 Heat oven to 350°F. Spray 3-cup shallow casserole with cooking spray. In 1-quart saucepan, melt butter over low heat. Stir in flour, salt, mustard and pepper. Cook over medium heat, stirring constantly, until mixture is smooth and bubbly; remove from heat. Gradually stir in milk. Heat to boiling, stirring constantly; boil and stir 1 minute. Remove from heat; stir in cheese until melted.

2 Pour half of the sauce into bottom of casserole. Arrange potato wedges over sauce in casserole. Pour remaining sauce over potatoes. Cover casserole with foil.

3 Bake 30 minutes. Uncover and bake 18 to 22 minutes longer or until top is light golden brown and potatoes are tender. Sprinkle with chives before serving.

1 Serving: Calories 360; Total Fat 14g (Saturated Fat 8g, Trans Fat 0g); Cholesterol 40mg; Sodium 530mg; Total Carbohydrate 45g (Dietary Fiber 4g); Protein 13g **Exchanges:** 3 Starch, ½ High-Fat Meat, 1½ Fat **Carbohydrate Choices:** 3

Swap It Gruyère cheese adds a complex flavor to the sauce, but other cheeses work too. Try shredded Swiss, Emmental or other cheese you may have on hand.

Let's Celebrate!

Not all celebrations require a roomful of people. Here are some great go-to menus for your special occasions for two. Whether it's a birthday, anniversary, cheering up a friend or holiday meal, these menus are sure to please.

ASIAN "TAKE-OUT" NIGHT

Fresh, fast and better than the local restaurant, see page on right

Thai Red Curry Shrimp Skillet (page 206)

Green Beans and Red Peppers (page 304)

Ice-Cream Sandwich Bites (page 347)

COMFORT-PLUS DINNER

When it's cold and you crave comfort food

White Bean Hummus (page 271) and veggie sticks

Barbecued Beef Shepherd's Pie (page 102)

Spinach salad

Triple Chocolate Skillet Brownie Sundae (page 316)

EASY, SATISFYING LUNCH

Delicious and simple—skip the drive-thru

California Kimchi Tuna Melts (page 194)

Apple slices

Carrot sticks

Chips

Giant Peanut Butter and Candy Cookie (page 313)

LAZY WEEKEND BREAKFAST

A morning to savor after a hard week

Bacon and Egg Naan Pizzas (page 234)

Banana Bread Muffins (page 279)

Fresh fruit

Coffee and orange juice

LIGHT AND EASY SUMMER HANGOUT

Eat outside and play a lawn game

Spicy Barbecue Chicken Flatbread Pizza (page 274)

Veggie Burgers with Caramelized Onions (page 153)

Cilantro Grilled Corn (page 302)

Pineapple-Mojito Sorbet (page 345)

ROMANTIC DINNER

Valentine's Day, an anniversary or date night

Italian Beef Kabobs (page 105)

Browned Butter Mashed Potatoes (page 289)

Broccoli with Pine Nuts (page 285)

Chocolate–Peanut Butter Lava Cakes (page 322)

STAY-IN MOVIE NIGHT

Fun munchies to enjoy on the sofa

Pimiento Cheese and Corn–Stuffed Mini Peppers (page 273)

Curried Beef Pizzas (page 92)

Ginger, Walnut and White Chocolate Cookies (page 311)

Beer and/or soda pop

BLT Poutine

Prep Time: 15 Minutes • Start to Finish: 30 Minutes • 2 servings

10   oz frozen French-fried potatoes (about 2½ cups)

1   cup yellow cheese curds (5 oz)

⅓   cup bottled Sriracha ranch dressing

½   cup shredded leaf lettuce

¼   cup crisply cooked, crumbled bacon

2   tablespoons chopped tomato

1 Bake potatoes as directed on package until crisp and golden brown. Turn oven off.

2 Spread hot potatoes on oven-safe serving plate. Sprinkle with cheese curds (break large curds in half). Return to warm oven 1 to 2 minutes or until cheese curds begin to soften.

3 Drizzle with dressing. Top with lettuce, bacon and tomato. Serve immediately.

1 Serving: Calories 610; Total Fat 38g (Saturated Fat 12g, Trans Fat 0.5g); Cholesterol 60mg; Sodium 1470mg; Total Carbohydrate 43g (Dietary Fiber 4g); Protein 22g **Exchanges:** 2½ Starch, ½ Other Carbohydrate, 2 Lean Meat, 6 Fat **Carbohydrate Choices:** 3

Swap It To make your own Sriracha ranch dressing, combine ⅓ cup regular ranch dressing with 1 teaspoon Sriracha sauce.

Swap It Waffle-fried potatoes or potato nuggets can be used in place of the French-fried potatoes.

Chutney Potato Salad

Prep Time: 30 Minutes • Start to Finish: 2 Hours 30 Minutes • 3 servings (⅔ cup each)

SALAD

- ¾ lb unpeeled small red potatoes, quartered
- ½ teaspoon salt
- ¼ cup frozen peas, cooked
- ¼ cup chopped orange bell pepper
- 2 tablespoons sliced green onions (2 medium)
- 1 tablespoon chopped fresh parsley

DRESSING

- 2 tablespoons mayonnaise
- 2 tablespoons plain Greek yogurt
- 2 tablespoons chutney
- 1 teaspoon curry powder
- ¼ teaspoon salt

1 Place potatoes in 2-quart saucepan; add enough water and salt just to cover potatoes. Cover and heat to boiling; reduce heat to low. Cook 8 to 10 minutes or until potatoes are tender; drain. Cool 10 minutes.

2 In medium bowl, stir together all dressing ingredients. Add potatoes and remaining salad ingredients; toss. Cover and refrigerate at least 2 hours but no longer than 24 hours.

1 Serving: Calories 190; Total Fat 7g (Saturated Fat 1g, Trans Fat 0g); Cholesterol 0mg; Sodium 700mg; Total Carbohydrate 27g (Dietary Fiber 3g); Protein 4g **Exchanges:** ½ Starch, 1 Other Carbohydrate, ½ Vegetable, 1½ Fat **Carbohydrate Choices:** 2

Kitchen Tip Curry powder is a mix of a variety of spices. Most Indian cooks make their own curry, with each recipe often being unique to the cook. You can purchase prepared curry in the spice aisle of the grocery store. Each brand will vary slightly, so adjust the level according to your own taste.

Use It Up Extra potatoes are terrific cut up and tossed in olive oil, salt and pepper and then roasted at 425°F about 30 minutes or until tender.

Creamy Parmesan Rice *with* Spinach

Prep Time: 10 Minutes • Start to Finish: 30 Minutes • 2 servings (¾ cup each)

1 tablespoon butter

½ cup uncooked regular long-grain white rice

2 tablespoons sliced green onions

½ teaspoon finely chopped garlic

½ cup water

½ cup milk

¼ teaspoon salt

1 cup coarsely chopped fresh spinach

2 tablespoons grated Parmesan cheese

Additional grated Parmesan cheese, if desired

1 In 1-quart saucepan, melt butter over medium heat. Stir in rice, green onions and garlic. Cook and stir 3 to 4 minutes or until rice is lightly toasted.

2 Stir in water, milk and salt. Heat to boiling; reduce heat. Cover and simmer about 20 minutes or until rice is tender. Stir in spinach and the 2 tablespoons of cheese. Cover and let stand 1 to 2 minutes or until spinach is wilted and cheese has melted. Gently stir before serving. Sprinkle with additional cheese.

1 Serving: Calories 300; Total Fat 9g (Saturated Fat 6g, Trans Fat 0g); Cholesterol 25mg; Sodium 480mg; Total Carbohydrate 45g (Dietary Fiber 1g); Protein 9g **Exchanges:** 2 Starch, 1 Other Carbohydrate, ½ Vegetable, 1½ Fat **Carbohydrate Choices:** 3

Kitchen Tip If rice is not tender and liquid is absorbed, stir in an additional tablespoon or two of water. Cover and cook on low heat until tender.

Swap It Feel free to use chopped chives instead of the green onions or fresh arugula instead of the spinach.

Butternut Squash *and* Leek Stuffing

Prep Time: 15 Minutes • Start to Finish: 45 Minutes • 3 servings (⅔ cup each)

3 tablespoons butter

¾ cup diced butternut squash (about 4 oz)

⅓ cup sliced leek

1½ cups seasoned salad croutons (from 5-oz bag)

2 tablespoons chopped fresh Italian (flat-leaf) parsley

⅓ cup chicken broth (from 32-oz carton)

3 tablespoons shredded Parmesan cheese

1 Heat oven to 350°F. Spray 20-ounce casserole dish with cooking spray. In 10-inch nonstick skillet, melt butter over medium heat. Stir in squash and leek; cook and stir 3 to 4 minutes or until leek is tender. Spoon into medium bowl; cool 5 minutes.

2 Add croutons, parsley and chicken broth to vegetable mixture; stir gently to mix well. Toss with Parmesan cheese.

3 Pour mixture into casserole dish; cover with foil.

4 Bake 15 minutes. Remove from oven; remove foil. Return to oven; bake, uncovered, an additional 15 minutes or until top is golden brown.

1 Serving: Calories 250; Total Fat 17g (Saturated Fat 10g, Trans Fat 1.5g); Cholesterol 35mg; Sodium 510mg; Total Carbohydrate 18g (Dietary Fiber 2g); Protein 5g **Exchanges:** 1 Starch, ½ Vegetable, 3½ Fat **Carbohydrate Choices:** 1

Kitchen Tip The vegetable mixture is cooled before adding the remaining ingredients so that the Parmesan cheese can be evenly distributed in the stuffing.

Swap It Use this stuffing in place of the prepared stuffing in the Sheet Pan Turkey Dinner (page 39). Prepare this recipe through Step 2 and continue as directed in Step 4 of the Sheet Pan Turkey Dinner recipe.

Cilantro Grilled Corn

Prep Time: 15 Minutes • Start to Finish: 15 Minutes • 2 servings

1 teaspoon finely chopped garlic

2 teaspoons finely chopped fresh cilantro

¼ teaspoon salt

Butter-flavored cooking spray

2 ears corn, husked

1 Heat gas or charcoal grill. In small bowl, mix garlic, cilantro and salt.

2 Cut two 12-inch square pieces of heavy-duty foil. Spray each ear of corn generously with cooking spray. Spread garlic mixture over each ear of corn. Wrap each ear of corn in foil piece, sealing edges. Allow space for circulation and expansion.

3 Cover and grill corn over medium heat 10 to 12 minutes, turning occasionally, until tender.

1 Serving: Calories 120; Total Fat 1.5g (Saturated Fat 0g, Trans Fat 0g); Cholesterol 0mg; Sodium 300mg; Total Carbohydrate 22g (Dietary Fiber 2g); Protein 3g **Exchanges:** 1 Starch, ½ Other Carbohydrate, ½ Vegetable **Carbohydrate Choices:** 1½

Kitchen Tip Use your fingers to spread the garlic mixture on the corn. It may be a little messy, but it's an easy way to evenly spread the mixture over the corn.

Asparagus Parmesan

Prep Time: 10 Minutes • Start to Finish: 10 Minutes • 2 servings (1 cup each)

1 box (9 oz) frozen asparagus cuts

1 cup sliced fresh mushrooms

2 teaspoons butter (do not use margarine)

⅛ teaspoon garlic powder

Freshly ground pepper

1 tablespoon grated Parmesan cheese

1 Remove asparagus from pouch; place in medium microwavable bowl. Microwave on High 2 minutes.

2 Stir in remaining ingredients except Parmesan cheese. Microwave 2 to 4 minutes longer, stirring occasionally, until asparagus is crisp-tender. Just before serving, sprinkle with Parmesan cheese.

1 Serving: Calories 90; Total Fat 5g (Saturated Fat 3g, Trans Fat 0g); Cholesterol 15mg; Sodium 85mg; Total Carbohydrate 4g (Dietary Fiber 2g); Protein 5g **Exchanges:** 1 Vegetable, ½ Lean Meat, ½ Fat **Carbohydrate Choices:** 0

Swap It If you're short on time or don't have fresh mushrooms on hand, use a 2.5-ounce jar of sliced mushrooms instead. Top this tasty side with shredded fresh Parmesan cheese, if you like, instead of the grated cheese.

Green Beans *and* Red Peppers

Prep Time: 20 Minutes • Start to Finish: 20 Minutes • 2 servings

8   oz fresh green beans, broken into 2-inch pieces (2 cups)

½   medium red bell pepper, cut into 2 × ¼-inch strips

1   tablespoon honey mustard

1 In 1½-quart saucepan, place beans in 1 inch water. Heat to boiling; reduce heat. Boil, uncovered, 5 minutes. Cover and boil 5 to 10 minutes longer or until beans are crisp-tender; drain.

2 Stir bell pepper and honey mustard into beans.

1 Serving: Calories 60; Total Fat 0.5g (Saturated Fat 0g, Trans Fat 0g); Cholesterol 0mg; Sodium 95mg; Total Carbohydrate 10g (Dietary Fiber 4g); Protein 2g **Exchanges:** 2 Vegetable **Carbohydrate Choices:** ½

Kitchen Tip Decrease your last-minute meal preparation time by prepping the beans and bell pepper in the morning, then storing them in the refrigerator.

Southern Hot Corn

Prep Time: 25 Minutes • Start to Finish: 45 Minutes • 2 servings (½ cup each)

1¼ cups frozen whole kernel corn

½ cup chopped red bell pepper

⅓ cup shredded Cheddar cheese

¼ cup spicy jalapeño cream cheese spread

2 tablespoons chopped fresh parsley

2 tablespoons milk

1 tablespoon butter

¼ teaspoon smoked paprika

Smoked paprika and chopped parsley, if desired

1 Spray 20-ounce casserole dish with nonstick cooking spray. Set oven control to broil. Line shallow pan with cooking parchment paper. Place corn and red pepper in single layer in pan.

2 Broil with tops of vegetables 6 inches from heat 12 to 16 minutes, stirring halfway through broiling, or until edges begin to brown. Remove from oven. Heat oven to 350°F.

3 In 1-quart saucepan, heat Cheddar cheese, cream cheese, parsley, milk, butter and paprika over medium heat 1 to 2 minutes, stirring constantly, or until cheese is melted. Stir in vegetables. Pour into casserole dish.

4 Bake 18 to 20 minutes or until hot and bubbly. Sprinkle with additional paprika and parsley.

1 Serving: Calories 330; Total Fat 21g (Saturated Fat 13g, Trans Fat 0.5g); Cholesterol 70mg; Sodium 340mg; Total Carbohydrate 25g (Dietary Fiber 3g); Protein 10g **Exchanges:** 1 Starch, ½ Other Carbohydrate, 1 High-Fat Meat, 2½ Fat **Carbohydrate Choices:** 1½

Swap It This dish doubles as an appetizer dip to serve alongside tortilla chips, crackers or slices of French bread.

Kitchen Tip If you can't find jalapeño cream cheese spread, use regular cream cheese spread and stir in 2 teaspoons finely chopped jalapeño chiles.

DESSERTS

Ginger, Walnut *and* White Chocolate Cookies

Prep Time: 10 Minutes • Start to Finish: 25 Minutes • 1 dozen cookies

- 6 tablespoons butter, softened
- ¼ cup granulated sugar
- ¼ cup packed brown sugar
- ¼ teaspoon vanilla
- 1 egg white
- 1 cup all-purpose flour
- ¼ teaspoon baking soda
- ¼ teaspoon salt
- 4 tablespoons finely chopped crystallized ginger
- 3 tablespoons white vanilla baking chips
- 3 tablespoons chopped walnuts

1 Heat oven to 350°F. In medium bowl, beat butter, granulated sugar and brown sugar with spoon until creamy. Stir in vanilla and egg white until well mixed. Stir in flour, baking soda and salt. Stir in 3 tablespoons of the crystallized ginger, the white vanilla baking chips and walnuts.

2 Drop dough by rounded tablespoonfuls about 2 inches apart onto large ungreased cookie sheet. Flatten slightly; sprinkle with remaining ginger. Bake 10 to 13 minutes or until edges are set and lightly browned. Cool 2 minutes; remove from cookie sheet to wire rack.

1 Cookie: Calories 170; Total Fat 8g (Saturated Fat 4.5g, Trans Fat 0g); Cholesterol 30mg; Sodium 135mg; Total Carbohydrate 21g (Dietary Fiber 0g); Protein 2g **Exchanges:** 1 Starch, ½ Other Carbohydrate, 1½ Fat **Carbohydrate Choices:** 1½

Kitchen Tip Crystallized ginger comes in different packages and shapes. It can be found in jars in the spice aisle, in packages in the produce section or sometimes in bulk bins.

Swap It Walnuts are delicious in this recipe, but pecans, macadamia nuts or almonds work too.

Giant Peanut Butter *and* Candy Cookie

Prep Time: 15 Minutes • Start to Finish: 35 Minutes • 4 servings

2 tablespoons butter, melted

2 tablespoons creamy peanut butter

¼ cup packed brown sugar

1 egg yolk

½ teaspoon vanilla

½ cup all-purpose flour

¼ teaspoon baking soda

¼ teaspoon salt

¼ cup candy-coated chocolate candies

1 Heat oven to 350°F. Spray cookie sheet with cooking spray. In medium bowl, mix butter, peanut butter and brown sugar with spoon until well blended. Add egg yolk and vanilla; stir about 30 seconds or until creamy. Add flour, baking soda and salt; stir until blended. Mix in candies using wooden spoon.

2 Shape dough into ball; place on cookie sheet. Flatten slightly with palm of hand to 6-inch round.

3 Bake 12 to 16 minutes or until golden brown. Cool 5 minutes; remove from cookie sheet to cooling rack. To serve, cut into quarters.

1 Serving: Calories 290; Total Fat 14g (Saturated Fat 7g, Trans Fat 0g); Cholesterol 60mg; Sodium 320mg; Total Carbohydrate 37g (Dietary Fiber 1g); Protein 4g **Exchanges:** 2½ Other Carbohydrate, ½ High-Fat Meat, 2 Fat **Carbohydrate Choices:** 2½

Kitchen Tip For best results, do not use "natural-style" peanut butter.

Cinnamon-Frosted Molasses Cookies

Prep Time: 15 Minutes • Start to Finish: 1 Hour • 1 dozen cookies

COOKIES

½	cup packed brown sugar
6	tablespoons butter, softened
2	tablespoons molasses
1	egg white
1	cup plus 2 tablespoons all-purpose flour
½	teaspoon baking soda
½	teaspoon ground cinnamon
½	teaspoon ground ginger
¼	teaspoon ground cloves
⅛	teaspoon salt

FROSTING

¾	cup powdered sugar
2	tablespoons butter, softened
¼	teaspoon ground cinnamon
2½ to 3½	teaspoons milk

1 Heat oven to 350°F. In medium bowl, beat brown sugar, butter, molasses and egg white with spoon or mixer until smooth. Stir in remaining cookie ingredients.

2 Shape dough into 1½-inch balls. Place balls about 2 inches apart on large ungreased cookie sheet.

3 Bake 11 to 13 minutes or just until set and cookies appear dry. Cool on cookie sheet 2 minutes. Remove from cookie sheet to cooling rack. Cool at least 30 minutes.

4 In small bowl, mix powdered sugar, butter and cinnamon with spoon. Stir in just enough milk to make frosting smooth and spreadable. Frost each cookie with about 1 teaspoon frosting.

1 Cookie: Calories 190; Total Fat 8g (Saturated Fat 5g, Trans Fat 0g); Cholesterol 20mg; Sodium 150mg; Total Carbohydrate 28g (Dietary Fiber 0g); Protein 1g **Exchanges:** 2 Other Carbohydrate, 1½ Fat **Carbohydrate Choices:** 2

Kitchen Tip For a fancy presentation, place frosting in resealable food-safe plastic bag. Snip end of bag and pipe frosting over cookies.

Kitchen Tip For traditional molasses crinkles, roll balls of dough in sugar. Place on cookie sheet. Bake as directed and omit frosting.

Triple Chocolate Skillet Brownie Sundae

Prep Time: 15 Minutes • Start to Finish: 40 Minutes • 4 servings

⅓ cup semisweet chocolate chips

¼ cup butter, softened

2 tablespoons sugar

¼ teaspoon vanilla

1 egg white

½ cup all-purpose flour

⅛ teaspoon baking soda

2 tablespoons milk chocolate chips

2 tablespoons white vanilla baking chips

1 cup ice cream (any flavor)

¼ cup chocolate or caramel syrup

1 Heat oven to 375°F. In small microwavable bowl, microwave chocolate chips on High 30 to 60 seconds, stirring after 30 seconds until chocolate is melted; stir until smooth. Cool slightly.

2 Meanwhile, in medium bowl, beat butter, sugar and vanilla with spoon until smooth and creamy. Stir in egg white, the melted chocolate, flour, baking soda, milk chocolate chips and white vanilla baking chips.

3 Spread dough in 6-inch ovenproof skillet. Bake 14 to 17 minutes or just until edges are set and toothpick inserted in center comes out with fudgy crumbs.

4 To serve, scoop warm brownie into 4 dessert bowls; top with ice cream and syrup.

1 Serving: Calories 440; Total Fat 23g (Saturated Fat 14g, Trans Fat 0.5g); Cholesterol 45mg; Sodium 200mg; Total Carbohydrate 54g (Dietary Fiber 2g); Protein 5g **Exchanges:** 1½ Starch, 2 Other Carbohydrate, 4½ Fat **Carbohydrate Choices:** 3½

Swap It Use peanut butter or butterscotch chips instead of the white vanilla baking chips, and stir in a tablespoon of chopped nuts, if desired, with the chips in step 3.

Swap It Instead of ice cream, top brownies with whipped cream and any variety of ice-cream topping. It's a whole new dessert.

Kitchen Tip Brownie can also be baked in an ungreased 8-inch ovenproof skillet. Bake 11 to 13 minutes.

Glazed Lemon-Coconut Bars

Prep Time: 15 Minutes • Start to Finish: 1 Hour 35 Minutes • 8 bars

BARS

- ⅔ cup plus 1½ teaspoons Easy Dessert Mix (page 325)
- 3 tablespoons firm butter
- ⅓ cup granulated sugar
- 2 tablespoons flaked coconut
- 1 teaspoon grated lemon peel
- 2 tablespoons lemon juice
- 1 tablespoon water
- 1 egg, slightly beaten

GLAZE

- ¼ cup powdered sugar
- 1½ teaspoons lemon juice

1 Heat oven to 350°F. Line bottom and long sides of 8 × 4-inch loaf pan with cooking parchment paper. In small bowl, place ⅔ cup of the Easy Dessert Mix. Cut in butter, using pastry blender or fork, until crumbly. Press in pan.

2 Bake 15 to 18 minutes or until light brown.

3 Meanwhile, in small bowl, mix remaining 1½ teaspoons Easy Dessert Mix and remaining bar ingredients. Pour coconut mixture over baked layer.

4 Bake 16 to 20 minutes longer or until set and light golden brown around edges. Cool on cooling rack about 1 hour.

5 In small bowl, stir all glaze ingredients until smooth; spread over bars. Sprinkle with additional coconut, if desired. For bars, cut into 4 rows by 2 rows.

1 Bar: Calories 180; Total Fat 6g (Saturated Fat 3.5g, Trans Fat 0g); Cholesterol 35mg; Sodium 120mg; Total Carbohydrate 30g (Dietary Fiber 0g); Protein 2g **Exchanges:** ½ Starch, 1½ Other Carbohydrate, 1 Fat **Carbohydrate Choices:** 2

Kitchen Tip You will need 1 lemon to get enough peel and juice for these bars.

Swap It Sprinkle the bars with powdered sugar instead of glazing the bars.

Spiced Pumpkin–Chocolate Chip Mug Cake

Prep Time: 10 Minutes • Start to Finish: 20 Minutes • 1 serving

CAKE

- 2 tablespoons butter
- ¼ cup (from 15-oz can) pumpkin (not pumpkin pie mix)
- 2 tablespoons milk
- ½ teaspoon vanilla
- ½ cup Easy Dessert Mix (page 325)
- ¼ teaspoon pumpkin pie spice
- 1 tablespoon miniature semisweet chocolate chips

TOPPING

- ¼ cup whipping cream
- 1 teaspoon powdered sugar
- ⅛ teaspoon pumpkin pie spice
- 1 tablespoon caramel topping
- 1 teaspoon miniature semisweet chocolate chips

1 In 12-ounce microwavable coffee mug, microwave butter on High 30 to 45 seconds or until melted. Stir in pumpkin, milk, vanilla, Easy Dessert Mix and ¼ teaspoon pumpkin spice with fork until well blended. Stir in 1 tablespoon of the miniature chocolate chips.

2 Microwave uncovered on High 1 to 2 minutes or until toothpick inserted in center comes out clean and cake pulls from sides of mug. Cool 5 minutes.

3 Meanwhile, in small bowl, beat whipping cream with electric mixer on medium speed until soft peaks form. Add powdered sugar and pinch of pumpkin pie spice; beat on medium speed until stiff peaks form. Spoon whipped topping onto cake. Drizzle with caramel topping. Sprinkle with 1 teaspoon miniature chocolate chips.

1 Serving: Calories 1180; Total Fat 48g (Saturated Fat 29g, Trans Fat 1.5g); Cholesterol 130mg; Sodium 900mg; Total Carbohydrate 174g (Dietary Fiber 5g); Protein 12g **Exchanges:** 4 Starch, 7½ Other Carbohydrate, 9 Fat **Carbohydrate Choices:** 11½

Kitchen Tip Make sure that the mug holds at least 12 ounces of liquid or cake may overflow.

Swap It Fresh whipped cream is divine, however, you can skip whipping cream and use a little whipped cream from an aerosol can, sprinkle with the pumpkin pie spice and drizzle with the caramel topping.

Chocolate–Peanut Butter Lava Cakes

Prep Time: 15 Minutes • Start to Finish: 30 Minutes • 2 servings

About 2 teaspoons unsweetened baking cocoa

⅓ cup plus 2 tablespoons bittersweet chocolate chips (from 10-oz package)

¼ cup butter (do not use margarine)

1 egg

½ cup powdered sugar

3 tablespoons all-purpose flour

Dash salt

4 teaspoons creamy peanut butter

Additional powdered sugar and cocoa, if desired

1 Heat oven to 425°F. Grease bottoms and sides of 2 (6-oz) custard cups or ramekins with shortening; sprinkle with unsweetened baking cocoa. Place custard cups on 12½x9½x1-inch pan.

2 In small microwavable bowl, melt ⅓ cup of the baking chips and the butter on High about 30 seconds or until mixture can be stirred smooth. Cool slightly.

3 In another small bowl, beat egg with whisk until well blended. Beat in ½ cup powdered sugar. Beat in melted chocolate mixture, flour and salt.

4 Spoon a scant ¼ cup batter into each custard cup. Spoon 2 teaspoons peanut butter and 1 tablespoon of the baking chips onto center of batter in each cup. Top each with remaining chocolate batter.

5 Bake 10 to 12 minutes or until top edges are set and centers are still soft. Let stand 3 minutes. Run small knife or metal spatula along sides of cakes to loosen. Place heatproof serving plate upside down over each cup. Carefully, turn plate and custard cup over. Remove custard cup. Sprinkle with additional powdered sugar and cocoa. Serve warm.

1 Serving: Calories 810; Total Fat 58g (Saturated Fat 33g, Trans Fat 1g); Cholesterol 155mg; Sodium 420mg; Total Carbohydrate 56g (Dietary Fiber 9g); Protein 14g **Exchanges:** 1 Starch, 2½ Other Carbohydrate, ½ Medium-Fat Meat, 1 High-Fat Meat, 9½ Fat **Carbohydrate Choices:** 4

Kitchen Tip Why coat the custard cups or ramekins with shortening and cocoa? Shortening thoroughly coats the inside of the cup and ensures that the cakes will release easily and completely from the cups. The cocoa helps as well but also adds to the darkness and richness of the cake crust.

Swap It If you have semisweet chocolate chips, use them in place of the bittersweet chocolate chips.

Cherry Cobblers

Prep Time: 10 Minutes • Start to Finish: 30 Minutes • 2 servings

1   cup cherry pie filling
    (from 21-oz can)

½   cup Easy Dessert Mix
    (page 325)

2   tablespoons milk

2   teaspoons butter,
    softened

    Sugar, if desired

1 Heat oven to 400°F. Divide pie filling between 2 (10-ounce) custard cups. Microwave on High 3 minutes or until heated; stir. Place custard cups on cookie sheet.

2 In small bowl, stir remaining ingredients until thick batter forms. Pour and spread evenly over pie filling in each custard cup. Sprinkle with sugar.

3 Bake 15 to 18 minutes or until topping is light brown.

1 Serving: Calories 340; Total Fat 4.5g (Saturated Fat 2.5g, Trans Fat 0g); Cholesterol 10mg; Sodium 190mg; Total Carbohydrate 71g (Dietary Fiber 2g); Protein 3g **Exchanges:** 1 Starch, 3½ Other Carbohydrate, 1 Fat **Carbohydrate Choices:** 5

Use It Up Use the remaining pie filling from the can as a topper for ice cream, pancakes or waffles.

Swap It You can use other pie fillings like apple or blueberry for the cobbler.

Easy Dessert Mix

Prep Time: 5 Minutes • Start to Finish: 5 Minutes

TO MAKE 2 CUPS DESSERT MIX

- 1⅓ cups all-purpose flour
- ¾ cup sugar
- 1¼ teaspoons baking powder
- ¼ teaspoon salt

TO MAKE 8 CUPS DESSERT MIX

- 5⅓ cups all-purpose flour
- 3 cups sugar
- 5 teaspoons baking powder
- 1 teaspoon salt

1 In medium or large bowl, mix ingredients for choice of either 2 cups cake mix or 8 cups cake mix until well blended.

2 Use immediately in this book calling for Easy Scratch Cake Mix. Or store in tightly covered container in cool, dark place for up to 1 month or freeze up to 3 months.

Kitchen Tip Use this recipe in several of the dessert recipes in this book, such as Cherry Cobblers (left).

Swap It Substitute brown sugar for the sugar.

Carrot Cake *with* Cream Cheese Frosting

Prep Time: 20 Minutes • Start to Finish: 1 Hour 40 Minutes • 4 servings

CAKE

- 1 cup Easy Dessert Mix (page 325)
- ½ teaspoon pumpkin pie spice
- ½ cup shredded carrot (about 1 medium)
- 3 tablespoons vegetable oil
- 2 tablespoons milk
- ½ teaspoon vanilla
- 1 egg
- 2 tablespoons raisins or dried currants
- 2 tablespoons chopped walnuts

FROSTING

- 1 tablespoon butter, softened
- 2 oz cream cheese, softened
- 1 cup powdered sugar
- ¼ teaspoon vanilla
- 1½ to 3 teaspoons milk

  Additional chopped walnuts and shredded carrot, if desired

1 Heat oven to 350°F. Spray 6-inch round cake pan with cooking spray. In medium bowl, stir together Easy Dessert Mix and pumpkin pie spice with spoon. Stir in remaining cake ingredients. Beat with spoon 1 minute; spread evenly in pan.

2 Bake 25 to 30 minutes or until toothpick inserted in center comes out clean. Cool 10 minutes. Carefully run small metal spatula or knife around side of pan to loosen cake; remove cake from pan. Cool completely, about 45 minutes.

3 In small bowl, beat butter and cream cheese with spoon until smooth; gradually beat in sugar, ¼ teaspoon vanilla and enough milk, 1 teaspoon at a time, until spreading consistency.

4 Frost top and side of cake with frosting. Garnish with additional chopped walnuts and shredded carrot. Store loosely covered in refrigerator.

1 Serving: Calories 510; Total Fat 22g (Saturated Fat 7g, Trans Fat 0g); Cholesterol 70mg; Sodium 250mg; Total Carbohydrate 72g (Dietary Fiber 1g); Protein 5g **Exchanges:** 1 Starch, 4 Other Carbohydrate, ½ High-Fat Meat, 3½ Fat **Carbohydrate Choices:** 5

Swap It Substitute ground cinnamon or apple pie spice for the pumpkin pie spice.

Kitchen Tip For a lovely presentation, drizzle cake with 1 tablespoon caramel topping just before serving.

Coconut Cream Pie Bites

Prep Time: 10 Minutes • Start to Finish: 6 Hours 10 Minutes • 4 mini pies

4   pecan shortbread cookies (from 11.3-oz package)

2   tablespoons sugar

1   tablespoon cornstarch

¾   cup milk

1   egg yolk, lightly beaten

¼   cup flaked or shredded coconut, toasted

1   tablespoon butter, softened

¼   teaspoon coconut extract

¼   cup whipped cream topping (from aerosol can) or frozen whipped topping, thawed

Additional toasted coconut, if desired

1 Place 1 cookie in each of 4 regular-size muffin cups; set aside.

2 In 1-quart saucepan, stir together sugar and cornstarch. Gradually stir in milk. Cook over medium heat, stirring constantly, just until mixture boils and thickens; boil and stir 1 minute. Remove from heat.

3 Stir about half the hot mixture into egg yolk. Gradually stir yolk mixture into hot mixture. Cook over medium heat, stirring constantly, just until mixture begins to bubble and is thickened. Remove from heat. Stir in coconut, butter and coconut extract.

4 Divide mixture among muffin cups (cups will be full); cover with plastic wrap. Refrigerate at least 6 hours or up to 24 hours.

5 To serve, run metal spatula or knife around pies to loosen; remove from pan to dessert plates. Top with whipped cream. Garnish with additional toasted coconut.

1 Mini Pie: Calories 220; Total Fat 13g (Saturated Fat 6g, Trans Fat 0g); Cholesterol 60mg; Sodium 115mg; Total Carbohydrate 23g (Dietary Fiber 0g); Protein 3g **Exchanges:** 1 Starch, ½ Other Carbohydrate, 2½ Fat **Carbohydrate Choices:** 1½

Kitchen Tip To toast coconut, bake, uncovered, in ungreased shallow pan at 350°F for 5 to 7 minutes, stirring occasionally, until golden brown. Or, cook in ungreased heavy skillet over medium-low heat 6 to 14 minutes, stirring frequently until browning begins, and then stirring constantly until golden brown.

Swap It Vanilla extract can be substituted for the coconut extract. The pies will have a milder coconut flavor.

Swap It Almond lovers can omit the coconut and coconut extract. Use almond extract instead. Top whipped cream with toasted sliced almonds.

Berry Pies

Prep Time: 10 Minutes • Start to Finish: 1 Hour • 2 mini pies

½ cup frozen unsweetened whole strawberries, thawed

⅓ cup frozen unsweetened blueberries, thawed

⅓ cup frozen unsweetened raspberries, thawed

3 tablespoons sugar

1 tablespoon cornstarch

1 refrigerated pie crust, softened as directed on box

1 egg white, beaten

½ teaspoon sugar

1 Heat oven to 425°F. In large bowl, mix berries, 3 tablespoons sugar and the cornstarch.

2 Divide berry mixture among 2 (6-ounce) custard cups or ramekins.

3 Unroll pie crust on work surface. Cut 2 (5-inch) rounds from pie crust. Place each round over pie filling, draping over edges of custard cups. Lightly brush pie crust with egg white. Cut slits on top of each. Sprinkle with ½ teaspoon sugar. Place custard cups on cookie sheet.

4 Bake 17 to 23 minutes or until edges are deep golden brown and centers are thoroughly baked. Cool about 30 minutes. Serve warm.

1 Mini Pie: Calories 640; Total Fat 28g (Saturated Fat 11g, Trans Fat 0g); Cholesterol 15mg; Sodium 610mg; Total Carbohydrate 92g (Dietary Fiber 5g); Protein 6g **Exchanges:** 2 Starch, 1 Fruit, 3 Other Carbohydrate, 5½ Fat **Carbohydrate Choices:** 6

Swap It If fresh berries are in season, they are a delightful substitute for the frozen!

Salted Caramel–Pecan Cheesecake

Prep Time: 10 Minutes • Start to Finish: 4 Hours 55 Minutes • 3 servings

CRUST

- 8 vanilla wafers (from 12-oz box)
- 2 tablespoons chopped pecans
- 1 tablespoon butter, melted

FILLING

- 3 tablespoons packed brown sugar
- 4 oz cream cheese, softened (from 8-oz package)
- 3 tablespoons sour cream
- ¼ teaspoon vanilla
- 1 egg white
- 2 tablespoons caramel topping

TOPPING

- 2 tablespoons chopped pecans
- 1 tablespoon caramel topping
- ⅛ teaspoon sea salt flakes

1 Heat oven to 350°F. Cut 12 × 6-inch piece of foil; fold in half to form square. Wrap outside bottom and side of 4½-inch springform pan with foil to prevent leaking.

2 Place crust ingredients in miniature food processor; process until finely ground. Press in bottom and ½ inch up side of pan.

3 Bake 8 minutes; remove from oven. Cool crust 10 minutes on wire rack. Reduce oven temperature to 300°F.

4 Meanwhile, in medium bowl, beat brown sugar and cream cheese with whisk until blended. Gradually beat in sour cream, vanilla and egg white until smooth. Spread 2 tablespoons caramel topping over bottom of crust. Pour cheese mixture into pan.

5 Bake 25 to 35 minutes or until cheesecake is just set. Turn oven off; open door 4 inches. Let cheesecake remain in oven 30 minutes. Run small metal spatula around edge of pan to loosen cheesecake. Cool in pan on wire rack 30 minutes. Cover loosely with waxed paper; refrigerate at least 3 hours or overnight.

6 To serve, run small metal spatula around edge of springform pan; carefully remove foil and side of pan. Sprinkle 2 tablespoons pecans over top of cheesecake, drizzle caramel topping over top and sprinkle with salt. Store covered in refrigerator.

1 Serving: Calories 420; Total Fat 28g (Saturated Fat 13g, Trans Fat 0.5g); Cholesterol 55mg; Sodium 380mg; Total Carbohydrate 37g (Dietary Fiber 1g); Protein 5g **Exchanges:** 2½ Other Carbohydrate, ½ High-Fat Meat, 5 Fat **Carbohydrate Choices:** 2½

Kitchen Tip The cream cheese mixture can be blended in the miniature processor too. Place all of the filling ingredients in the bowl and process until smooth.

Kitchen Tip Chop up one of your favorite chocolate-caramel-flavor candy bars and sprinkle over cheesecake.

Impossibly Easy Mocha Fudge Cheesecakes

Prep Time: 15 Minutes • Start to Finish: 3 Hours 5 Minutes • 3 servings

CHEESECAKES

- 1 teaspoon instant coffee granules or crystals
- 1 tablespoon coffee liqueur or cold strong brewed coffee
- 6 oz cream cheese (from 8-oz package), softened
- ¼ cup Original Bisquick mix
- ¼ cup sugar
- ¼ tsp vanilla
- 1 egg
- 1 oz semisweet baking chocolate, melted and cooled

TOPPING

- 1 tablespoon powdered sugar
- 1 teaspoon coffee liqueur, if desired
- ⅓ cup sour cream
- ¼ teaspoon vanilla

  Baking chocolate for chocolate shavings

1 Heat oven to 350°F. Spray 3 (10-ounce) custard cups with cooking spray. In small bowl, stir coffee and liqueur until coffee is dissolved. In another small bowl, beat coffee mixture, cream cheese, Bisquick mix, sugar, vanilla, egg and chocolate with electric mixer on high speed 1 minute. Spoon into custard cups. Place custard cups on ungreased cookie sheet.

2 Bake 18 to 20 minutes or until center is firm and puffed. Cool 5 minutes (top of cheesecake may be cracked).

3 In small bowl, stir powdered sugar, liqueur, sour cream and vanilla until blended. Carefully spread over cheesecakes. Cool 30 minutes. Refrigerate at least 2 hours or until chilled. Sprinkle with chocolate shavings before serving. Store covered in refrigerator.

1 Serving: Calories 460; Total Fat 30g (Saturated Fat 17g, Trans Fat 1g); Cholesterol 135mg; Sodium 300mg; Total Carbohydrate 38g (Dietary Fiber 1g); Protein 7g **Exchanges:** 1½ Other Carbohydrate, 1 Milk, 4½ Fat **Carbohydrate Choices:** 2½

Apple Crisp

Prep Time: 15 Minutes • Start to Finish: 45 Minutes • 2 servings

TOPPING

- ¼ cup all-purpose flour
- ⅓ cup old-fashioned oats
- 2 tablespoons packed brown sugar
- ¼ teaspoon ground cinnamon
- 2 tablespoons butter, melted

FILLING

- 2 medium apples, peeled, cored, diced (1½ cups)
- 1 tablespoon packed brown sugar
- 1 tablespoon all-purpose flour
- ¼ teaspoon ground cinnamon
- ⅛ teaspoon salt
- 1 tablespoon dried cranberries

1 Heat oven to 350°F. Spray 2 (10-ounce) custard cups with cooking spray. In medium bowl, mix all topping ingredients except butter. With fork, mix in melted butter until crumbly.

2 In another medium bowl, mix all filling ingredients. Divide filling evenly between custard cups. Top each with half of the topping. (Topping will settle during baking.)

3 Bake 25 to 30 minutes or until apples are tender and topping is brown. Serve warm.

1 Serving: Calories 350; Total Fat 13g (Saturated Fat 7g, Trans Fat 0g); Cholesterol 30mg; Sodium 260mg; Total Carbohydrate 56g (Dietary Fiber 3g); Protein 4g **Exchanges:** 1½ Starch, ½ Fruit, 1½ Other Carbohydrate, 2½ Fat **Carbohydrate Choices:** 4

Swap It Stir in 1 teaspoon orange peel to add a bright citrus taste to the apple filling.

Personal Bread Puddings *with* Caramel-Whiskey Sauce

Prep Time: 10 Minutes • Start to Finish: 20 Minutes • 2 servings

BREAD PUDDINGS

- 1½ cups ½-inch cubes day-old bread
- 2 tablespoons dried cranberries, cherries, blueberries or raisins
- ½ cup milk
- 1 egg
- 2 tablespoons packed brown sugar

CARAMEL-WHISKEY SAUCE

- 2 tablespoons caramel ice-cream topping
- 2 teaspoons whiskey, brandy or rum
- ⅛ teaspoon ground cinnamon

  Additional ground cinnamon, if desired

1 Divide bread cubes and cranberries between 2 (10-ounce) microwavable custard cups or 2 (10- to 12-ounce) microwavable mugs.

2 In small bowl, mix milk, egg and sugar with whisk until blended. Pour evenly over bread mixture; let stand 5 minutes to allow milk mixture to soak into bread.

3 Microwave uncovered on Medium (50%) about 4½ minutes or just until pudding is set. Cool 5 minutes.

4 Meanwhile, in small microwavable bowl, stir together caramel topping, whiskey and cinnamon. Microwave on High 15 seconds or until warm. Spoon over bread pudding. Sprinkle with additional cinnamon.

1 Serving: Calories 250; Total Fat 6g (Saturated Fat 2.5g, Trans Fat 0g); Cholesterol 100mg; Sodium 200mg; Total Carbohydrate 40g (Dietary Fiber 1g); Protein 7g **Exchanges:** 1½ Starch, 1 Other Carbohydrate, ½ Medium-Fat Meat, ½ Fat **Carbohydrate Choices:** 2½

Swap It While day-old French bread is traditional in bread pudding, use whatever kind you have on hand, such as cinnamon-raisin bread, whole wheat or multi-grain.

Kitchen Tip Bread pudding is actually more of a custard, with its high ratio of egg to milk. To make sure the custard sets, check for doneness by seeing that it is set, a knife inserted in center comes out clean or the internal temperature reaches 160°F.

Swap It For a different spin, omit the Caramel-Whiskey Sauce and top with a scoop of ice cream or a dollop of whipped cream.

Layered Berry-Yogurt Parfaits

Prep Time: 10 Minutes • Start to Finish: 10 Minutes • 2 servings

2   containers (4 oz each)
    Greek honey
    vanilla yogurt

⅔   cup original bran cereal
    shreds

½   cup fresh raspberries

½   cup fresh blueberries

1 Divide 1 container of yogurt between 2 parfait or clear drinking glasses.

2 Top each with 2½ tablespoons cereal, 2 tablespoons raspberries and 2 tablespoons blueberries. Repeat with remaining yogurt, cereal and berries. Serve immediately.

1 Serving: Calories 220; Total Fat 1g (Saturated Fat 0g, Trans Fat 0g); Cholesterol 0mg; Sodium 150mg; Total Carbohydrate 40g (Dietary Fiber 12g); Protein 11g **Exchanges:** 1 Starch, ½ Fruit, 1 Other Carbohydrate, ½ Skim Milk, ½ Very Lean Meat **Carbohydrate Choices:** 2½

Swap It You can use other fruits in this parfait. Try strawberries, bananas or sliced peaches.

Brandy–Pumpkin Pie Milkshakes

Prep Time: 10 Minutes • Start to Finish: 10 Minutes • 2 servings

2 cups vanilla ice cream, slightly softened

3 tablespoons brandy

2 tablespoons milk

¼ teaspoon pumpkin pie spice or ground cinnamon

⅛ slice cold baked pumpkin pie, cut into chunks (from 9-inch pie)

Sweetened whipped cream, if desired

Cinnamon sticks, if desired

1 In blender, place ice cream, brandy, milk and pumpkin pie spice. Cover and blend on high speed until smooth and creamy. Add pie chunks; cover and blend until smooth, stopping blender to scrape down sides if necessary.

2 Pour into 2 glasses; top with sweetened whipped cream and garnish with cinnamon stick. Serve immediately.

1 Serving: Calories 350; Total Fat 15g (Saturated Fat 9g, Trans Fat 0.5g); Cholesterol 65mg; Sodium 130mg; Total Carbohydrate 34g (Dietary Fiber 1g); Protein 5g **Exchanges:** ½ Starch, 1½ Other Carbohydrate, ½ Low-Fat Milk, 2½ Fat **Carbohydrate Choices:** 2

Pineapple-Mojito Sorbet

Prep Time: 10 Minutes • Start to Finish: 6 Hours 10 Minutes • 3 servings (⅔ cup each)

2 cups chopped fresh pineapple

½ cup water

½ cup sugar

1 tablespoon chopped fresh mint leaves

Additional chopped fresh pineapple or other fresh fruit and chopped mint, if desired

1 In blender, combine pineapple, water, sugar and mint. Blend thoroughly until smooth; transfer mixture to ungreased 8 × 4-inch loaf pan.

2 Freeze 4 to 6 hours or until firm, stirring several times during first 2 hours to keep mixture smooth. To serve, spoon into dessert dishes. Top with fresh fruit; garnish with additional mint. (Mixture can be frozen overnight without stirring, but will have an icier consistency. Remove from freezer and let stand at room temperature 10 to 15 minutes for easier scooping and better texture.)

1 Serving: Calories 200; Total Fat 0g (Saturated Fat 0g, Trans Fat 0g); Cholesterol 0mg; Sodium 0mg; Total Carbohydrate 48g (Dietary Fiber 1g); Protein 0g **Exchanges:** 1 Fruit, 2 Other Carbohydrate **Carbohydrate Choices:** 3

Swap It Fresh pineapple chunks can be purchased in the fruit section of the grocery store, making this an easy shortcut for dessert prep. Canned pineapple may also be substituted.

Kitchen Tip Serve as a slushy drink with sparkling water. Or add a half shot of rum for a slushy cocktail.

Ice-Cream Sandwich Bites

Prep Time: 15 Minutes • Start to Finish: 1 Hour 15 Minutes • 4 sandwich bites

1 container (3.6 oz) ice cream (½ cup)

8 thin creme-filled chocolate sandwich cookies (from 10.1-oz package)

½ cup semisweet chocolate chips

1 tablespoon shortening

2 teaspoons finely chopped pecans or walnuts

1 Let ice cream stand at room temperature for about 5 minutes to soften slightly. Line small cookie sheet with cooking parchment paper.

2 Place 4 cookies on cookie sheet. With small scoop or spoon, place about 2 tablespoons ice cream on top of each cookie. Place remaining cookies over ice cream. Press lightly. Run knife or thin metal spatula around ice cream to fill in gaps between cookies. Freeze uncovered at least 1 hour or until ice cream is firm.

3 In small microwavable bowl, microwave chocolate and shortening 30 to 60 seconds, stirring after 30 seconds until chocolate is melted and smooth.

4 Using tongs or fork, dip each cookie sandwich in chocolate mixture to coat. Return to cookie sheet. Sprinkle top with nuts. Place in freezer until ready to serve. Freeze any remaining sandwiches in tightly covered container up to 1 week.

1 Sandwich Bite: Calories 300; Total Fat 17g (Saturated Fat 7g, Trans Fat 0g); Cholesterol 5mg; Sodium 110mg; Total Carbohydrate 34g (Dietary Fiber 2g); Protein 2g **Exchanges:** ½ Starch, 1½ Other Carbohydrate, 3½ Fat **Carbohydrate Choices:** 2

Swap It Sprinkle tops of sandwiches with candy sprinkles, decors or shots instead of the nuts.

Metric Conversion Guide

U.S. UNITS	CANADIAN METRIC	AUSTRALIAN METRIC
¼ teaspoon	1 mL	1 ml
½ teaspoon	2 mL	2 ml
1 teaspoon	5 mL	5 ml
1 tablespoon	15 mL	20 ml
¼ cup	50 mL	60 ml
⅓ cup	75 mL	80 ml
½ cup	125 mL	125 ml
⅔ cup	150 mL	170 ml
¾ cup	175 mL	190 ml
1 cup	250 mL	250 ml
1 quart	1 liter	1 liter
1½ quarts	1.5 liters	1.5 liters
2 quarts	2 liters	2 liters
2½ quarts	2.5 liters	2.5 liters
3 quarts	3 liters	3 liters
4 quarts	4 liters	4 liters

U.S. UNITS	CANADIAN METRIC	AUSTRALIAN METRIC
1 ounce	30 grams	30 grams
2 ounces	55 grams	60 grams
3 ounces	85 grams	90 grams
4 ounces (¼ pound)	115 grams	125 grams
8 ounces (½ pound)	225 grams	225 grams
16 ounces (1 pound)	455 grams	500 grams
1 pound	455 grams	0.5 kilogram

NOTE: The recipes in this cookbook have not been developed or tested using metric measures. When converting recipes to metric, some variations in quality may be noted.

INCHES	CENTIMETERS
1	2.5
2	5.0
3	7.5
4	10.0
5	12.5
6	15.0
7	17.5
8	20.5
9	23.0
10	25.5
11	28.0
12	30.5
13	33.0

FAHRENHEIT	CELSIUS
32°	0°
212°	100°
250°	120°
275°	140°
300°	150°
325°	160°
350°	180°
375°	190°
400°	200°
425°	220°
450°	230°
475°	240°
500°	260°

Index

Page numbers in *italics* indicate illustrations

Recipe Testing and Calculating Nutrition Information

RECIPE TESTING:

- Large eggs and 2% milk were used unless otherwise indicated.

- Fat-free, low-fat, low-sodium or lite products were not used unless indicated.

- No nonstick cookware and bakeware were used unless otherwise indicated. No dark-colored, black or insulated bakeware was used.

- When a pan is specified, a metal pan was used; a baking dish or pie plate means ovenproof glass was used.

- An electric hand mixer was used for mixing only when mixer speeds are specified.

CALCULATING NUTRITION:

- The first ingredient was used wherever a choice is given, such as ⅓ cup sour cream or plain yogurt.

- The first amount was used wherever a range is given, such as 3- to 3½-pound whole chicken.

- The first serving number was used wherever a range is given, such as 4 to 6 servings.

- "If desired" ingredients were not included.

- Only the amount of a marinade or frying oil that is absorbed was included.